C000265105

Your
Horoscope
2023

....

Taurus

21 April – 21 May

igloobooks

Published in 2022
First published in the UK by Igloo Books Ltd
An imprint of Igloo Books Ltd
Cottage Farm, NN6 0BJ, UK
Owned by Bonnier Books
Sveavägen 56, Stockholm, Sweden
www.igloobooks.com

Copyright © 2022 Igloo Books Ltd

All rights reserved. No part of this publication may be
reproduced or transmitted in any form or by any means,
electronic, or mechanical, including photocopying, recording,
or by any information storage and retrieval system,
without permission in writing from the publisher.

0722 001
2 4 6 8 10 9 7 5 3 1
ISBN 978-1-80108-407-9

Written by Sally Kirkman
Additional content by Belinda Campbell and Denise Evans

Designed by Richard Sykes
Edited by Suzanne Fossey

Printed and manufactured in China

CONTENTS

. . . .

INTRODUCTION

. . . .

This 15-month guide has been designed and written to give a concise and accessible insight into both the nature of your star sign and the year ahead. Divided into two main sections, the first section of this guide will give you an overview of your character in order to help you understand how you think, perceive the world and interact with others and – perhaps just as importantly – why. You'll soon see that your zodiac sign is not just affected by a few stars in the sky, but by planets, elements, and a whole host of other factors, too.

The second section of this guide is made up of daily forecasts. Use these to increase your awareness of what might appear on your horizon, so that you're better equipped to deal with the days ahead. While this should never be used to dictate your life, it can be useful to see how your energies might be affected or influenced, which in turn can help you prepare for what life might throw your way.

By the end of these 15 months, these two sections should have given you a deeper understanding and awareness of yourself and, in turn, the world around you. There are never any definite certainties, but with an open mind you will find guidance for what might be, and learn to take more control of your own destiny.

THE CHARACTER OF THE BULL

· · · · · · · · · · · · · · · · · ·

Steady and grounded, Taurus is a fixed earth sign that the rest of the zodiac can surely rely on. Slow and steady is how this Bull wins the race. Those who have a Taurean in their life should learn to not expect fast results. But boy, when a Taurean delivers, it is likely to be a stunning result. Taurus is known for being one of the most multitalented signs in the zodiac calendar, with a keen eye for the aesthetic. Some of the best artists, makers, writers and creators the world has ever known have been Taureans, such as Salvador Dalí and William Shakespeare.

Lovers of the finer things in life, Taureans may want to surround themselves with beautiful soft furnishings, sparkling jewellery, alluring artwork and other riches. Likewise, Taureans will gorge themselves on equally fine wines and delicious foods. The lure of beautiful things can be constant for Taureans, and whilst this can feel like a cruel fate when money is not free flowing, it can be an added motivation for doggedly pursuing their goals. Perseverance, after all, is what this sign is also best known for. The Taurean love of beauty does not always stop with material things. This springtime sign has a deep connection with Mother Earth. Hiking and working outdoors to enjoy the beauty of the world or finding ways to preserve and protect nature's wonders can be integral to Taureans. The associated colour for Taurus is green, and whilst this may be linked to a love of nature, it can also be an indicator of a green-eyed monster that lies within. Possession is a key characteristic of the Bull, and whilst this usually relates to material objects, Taureans can sometimes be guilty of treating their loved ones as possessions too. Jealousy, superficiality and stubbornness are the potential downsides of the talented, nurturing and tenacious Taurean.

THE BULL

Strong and masculine, the Bull inside of Taurus has plenty of charge and direction – there's a reason why everyone aims for the bullseye! The Bull is capable of charging when necessary, similarly Taureans can roll up their sleeves and deliver solid and fast results when life demands it. However, like the Bull, Taureans are more suited to a slower pace of life. Stopping to smell the flowers, taking time to relax in green pastures; this instinct of appreciating Mother Earth should be indulged whenever possible. This sign has an utmost appreciation for the finer things in life, but too often this is translated into material objects and wealth alone. What Taureans value and benefit from most is a long meander through woodlands or reading a good book in the park. Taureans can be accused of being bullish or stubborn, particularly when change is happening that they are uncomfortable with, or if it feels too great or sudden. In ancient Greek mythology, Zeus transformed himself into a white bull and whisked his love, Europa, to Crete. Zeus's bull has many similarities with Taureans; romantic, tenacious, sometimes possessive and often mystical. Ultimately, the friends and family of a Taurean should feel safe with the Bull by their side, an utmost nurturing and protective symbol that slowly but steadily provides for loved ones.

VENUS

Venus is named after the Roman goddess of love and beauty, so it's no surprise that these very two things govern Taurus. Taureans can happily spend a night at the theatre, ballet or opera, nestled in plush, red velvet seats and revelling in some of the finest displays of beauty and culture with a glass of fine wine. Slaves to their senses, Taureans can take immense pleasure in music, art, dining and, last but not least, physical activities. Encouraged by Venus, tactile Taureans can have a reputation for being sensual lovers. Considered to be some of the most attractive people, guided by their desires and ruled by the planet of love, romance is likely to play a huge role in the life of a Taurean.

ELEMENTS, MODES AND POLARITIES

Each sign is made up of a unique combination of three defining groups: elements, modes and polarities. Each of these defining parts can manifest themselves in good and bad ways and none should be seen as a positive or a negative – including the polarities! Just like a jigsaw puzzle, piecing these groups together can help illuminate why each sign has certain characteristics and help us find a balance.

ELEMENTS

Fire: Dynamic and adventurous, signs with fire in them can be extroverted. Others are naturally drawn to them because of the positive light they give off, as well as their high levels of energy and confidence.

Earth: Signs with the earth element are steady and driven with their ambitions. They make for a solid friend, parent or partner due to their grounded influence and nurturing nature.

Air: The invisible element that influences each of the other elements significantly, air signs will provide much-needed perspective to others with their fair thinking, verbal skills and key ideas.

Water: Warm in the shallows and sometimes freezing as ice, this mysterious element is essential to the growth of everything around it through its emotional depth and empathy.

MODES

Cardinal: Pioneers of the calendar, cardinal signs jump-start each season and are the energetic go-getters.

Fixed: Marking the middle of the calendar, fixed signs firmly denote and value steadiness and reliability.

Mutable: As the seasons end, the mutable signs adapt and give themselves over gladly to the promise of change.

POLARITIES

Positive: Typically extroverted, positive signs take physical action and embrace outside stimulus in their life.

Negative: Usually introverted, negative signs value emotional development and experiencing life from the inside out.

TAURUS IN BRIEF

The table below shows the key attributes of Taureans. Use it for quick reference and to understand more about this fascinating sign.

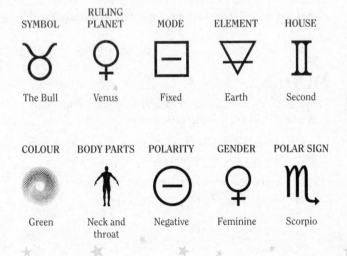

SYMBOL	RULING PLANET	MODE	ELEMENT	HOUSE
The Bull	Venus	Fixed	Earth	Second

COLOUR	BODY PARTS	POLARITY	GENDER	POLAR SIGN
Green	Neck and throat	Negative	Feminine	Scorpio

ROMANTIC RELATIONSHIPS

. . . .

The slow and steady nature of Taureans means that quick-fire love affairs are unlikely. Instead, they are more likely to find romance blossoming from a friendship, or pursue someone who has been on the outskirts of their life for a while. A sense of security is important to Taureans for their relationships to succeed. An insecure Taurean can turn into a jealous creature that is guilty of suffocating a relationship in a misguided effort to greedily possess a partner. Perhaps the most important lesson for this Bull is to learn how to share a partner's time rather then attempt to dominate it. This is not always an easy task for Taureans, particularly if they come from a small family and are less used to sharing their loved ones. Yet it's an important lesson to practise regularly to keep significant others happy. As with most things, sharing can be easier said than done. Communicating emotions is essential to any successful relationship, and will lead to deeper affection between Taureans and their loved ones.

An ideal partner for a Taurean is one that feeds both the desires and the stomach! Food is essential to the happiness of a Taurean, so the trick to keeping this relationship sweet may be to keep those snack drawers well stocked. A partner who cooks is one that a Taurean will be more inclined to try and keep hold of. Whilst Taureans love to be doted on and thrive on affection from their spouse, they should not be pandered to. A good partner for a Taurean should maintain a level of autonomy and not be tempted to indulge in letting their lover take ownership over them – even if it makes for an easier life! A Taurean's equal should fight to keep their

11

individuality, but also display patience and love. In return, a Taurean will show fierce loyalty and love, for better or for worse.

ARIES: COMPATIBILITY 3/5

The Taurean Bull and the Arean Ram may look like two headstrong individuals doomed to clash, but they actually have the potential for a sensual relationship. Whilst their passions for each other are intense, this couple will need to keep a reign on their potential stubbornness and desire to win in order to form a lasting relationship outside of the sheets. The Taurean can be guilty of possessiveness, which the free-spirited Arean may struggle with. However, with a joint love of nature and being outdoors, this passionate duo could find their Eden together.

TAURUS: COMPATIBILITY 4/5

This love can be one for the ages. When a Taurean falls for a Taurean, it may be slow and steady, as is their usual way, or it can be love, and lust, at first sight. These two romantics will shower each other with affection and reciprocate the dedication and loyalty that each deserves. Not ones to give up, both Bulls will stand by the other through thick and thin. Should they not see eye to eye, these two are capable of fighting with terrifying passion, but will hopefully find that making up is always more fun.

GEMINI: COMPATIBILITY 2/5

Three may prove to be a crowd. The duality of a Geminian, characterised in their twin symbol, can make a Taurean feel uneasy in starting a romantic relationship with this sign. The earth sign of Taurus mixed with airy Gemini may not be an easy joining, but if Taurus can budge on their fixed ways then love could grow happily here. Gemini's good communication skills will mean that they should hopefully understand quickly the needs of a Taurus and provide the love and security that Taureans crave in a partner. Communication, trust and flexibility should be this couple's mantra.

CANCER: COMPATIBILITY 5/5

Placed two positions apart on the zodiac calendar, a Cancerian and Taurean share a bond that can feel like home. The Cancerian's frequent displays of love are deep and clear, like two names carved into a tree! The intensity of the Taurean's affection, mixed with the Cancerian's head-over-heels approach, can see these two lovers running to the altar and settling down – not always in that order. Here are two signs that will do anything for each other, and will usually prefer their own little party of two.

LEO: COMPATIBILITY 3/5

Leo is ruled by the Sun and Taurus by Venus; this star and planet are never further than 48 degrees away from each other. The love that these two share is solidified in their sometimes stubborn commitment to one another. The Lion and Bull are both fixed signs and this can be their undoing in a long-term relationship if neither one is willing to compromise. Both will shower each other with affection and admiration, boost each other's self-esteem and be a positive influence in their careers. This couple should just be careful not to let their egos get in the way.

VIRGO: COMPATIBILITY 3/5

A Taurean and Virgoan can make for a real power couple. The Taurean's dogged approach to fulfilling goals and the Virgoan's practical and busy mind will see this pair securing a successful future together. The Virgoan can appear overly critical and may end up hurting the Bull's feelings unintentionally. Ruled by Mercury, the planet of communication, the Virgoan can be very attuned to the Taurean's needs and will try to fix any problems within the relationship. These two earth signs will likely share many things in common and can form lifelong companionships, even if a whirlwind romance isn't in the stars.

LIBRA: COMPATIBILITY 4/5

Both ruled by the planet Venus, the love that a Taurean and Libran share can be a thing of beauty. Their shared appreciation of culture and aesthetics will have romance blooming quickly. Wedding bells might ring in both the Taurean and Libran's ears, and planning for the big day could begin sooner rather than later. The Libran's airy indecisiveness can be a point of contention for the grounded Taurean, and these two won't be without their disagreements. However, the Libran's diplomacy will help to resolve issues and have them striving for harmony once more.

SCORPIO: COMPATIBILITY 5/5

Scorpio and Taurus are each other's opposites on the zodiac calendar, they therefore cosmically share a special relationship both in their differences and similarities. The element of Taurus is earth and Scorpio's is water, which usually will mean that both partners will provide something that the other desperately needs. Love and passion are both driving forces for these two. Scorpio has the reputation for being the most amorous of the signs and Taurus the most beautiful, so a physical relationship should be strong here. Whilst this couple will no doubt enjoy a close and passionate partnership, their tendencies towards more negative emotions will need to be kept in check.

SAGITTARIUS: COMPATIBILITY 2/5

A Sagittarian is ruled by the planet Jupiter, which is associated with luck – something that a Taurean doesn't always believe in. Whilst the Sagittarian values new experiences, the Taurean prefers familiar, safer comforts. The biggest struggle that this fire and earth couple may have is the Sagittarian's need for freedom and the Taurean's tendency towards possessiveness with a partner. A claustrophobic atmosphere should be avoided and freedom actively given in this relationship. They must learn from one another; both by admiring the faster gallop of the Centaur and equally by appreciating the steady plod of the Bull.

CAPRICORN: COMPATIBILITY 3/5

A Capricornian and Taurean in love are loyal and true to each other. These two earth signs value hard work, and are driven by their need to enjoy the fruits of their labours. The home that these two could build together will likely be full of beautiful and expensive objects, with a couple of prized cars jewelling the garage. Whilst both will have dreams of marriage, the Capricornian is the more traditional one and will probably approach the subject first. The Taurean should try to inject joy and fun into the relationship to teach the Capricornian how to enjoy the lighter side of life.

AQUARIUS: COMPATIBILITY 1/5

A Taurean and Aquarian aren't an obvious match on paper, and it's unlikely they will be paired on a dating website. The core differences between these two make a romantic spark unlikely, but should not be ruled out. The Aquarian is partly ruled by the planet Uranus, symbolising rebellion and change – often the Taurean's worst nightmare. For the easy-life-seeking Taurean who likes what they know, the Aquarian's wanderlust can be hard to keep up with. These two signs are both fixed and have the potential to make each other stronger if they remain open to change.

PISCES: COMPATIBILITY 3/5

A Taurean and Piscean are capable of having a highly sympathetic and understanding love together. The practical-minded Taurean should encourage the dreamy Piscean to live out fantasies and work hard, for everyone's benefit. In return, the Piscean will shower the Taurean in waves of love and gratitude for all the support and encouragement. However, the Piscean would be wise to not saturate the relationship emotionally and spoil the Taurean. With the Piscean being a water sign, the Taurean can feel the nourishing effects this sign has on its earth element, and the life that these two can grow together is one well worth living.

FAMILY AND FRIENDS

. . . .

Just as Taureans are dedicated to sticking to their goals, the same steadfast dedication is given to maintaining relationships with friends and family. Taureans want to see loved ones succeed, and will try to offer unfailing support mentally, physically and financially if they can. Positioned under the second house in the zodiac calendar, Taurus has a strong influence with possessions and money. Taureans are not ones to spend all their hard-earned wealth on just themselves, instead they are likely to want to share their fortunes with loved ones. From picking up a cheque for dinner to paying for extracurricular activities for their children, Taureans are generous with their love, time and money.

A Taurean home will clearly display signs of success, wealth and a love for beautiful and opulent design. From decorative throws and pillows, to the artwork hanging on the walls (that may or may not be a Taurean original), to the grand piano taking centre stage, the Taurean home will likely be a stunning display of the beauty in life. Beauty-loving Librans and homemaking Cancerians will value the stylish home that Taureans are capable of building, and can provide some of the most appreciative and kindred of friendships or relatives.

A key characteristic of Taureans is their focus on possession, which can lead them to become workaholics in their desire to be the affluent provider for their family. When it comes to family, it's important for Taureans to remember that the people for whom they are providing are more important than what they are providing. Despite their weakness for possession, what Taureans are more reliably known for is their unmoving loyalty and stability, both key attributes for building a happy family home. If a Taurean befriends or is related to another Taurean, their relationship will have the strong bones for forming some of the most reliable and steady relationships that the zodiac calendar knows.

Be careful of upsetting Taureans because they can hold a grudge for years and years. They would do well to learn to forgive any friends and family they feel have done them an injustice, if they want to keep that person in their life. Taureans should ask themselves this question: is it more important to hold on to this grudge or to hold on to this relationship? Taureans choose their friendships wisely and will usually be unwilling to let go of their investment in them, even if the friendship has soured or become too toxic to remain close. Taureans should learn to live and let live, and move forwards from any disagreements that they have with their family and friends. If a Taurean chooses to keep a friendship after a falling out, it should be based on forgiveness with an unclouded look towards a happier, shared future.

MONEY AND CAREERS

. . . .

Being a particular star sign will not dictate certain types of career, but it can help identify potential areas for thriving in. Conversely, to succeed in the workplace, it is just as important to understand strengths and weaknesses to achieve career and financial goals.

The mode of Taurus is fixed, rather than cardinal or mutable, which in career terms can mean that once Taureans decide what their career path is, they will stubbornly stick with it until they achieve their goal ambitions. Which career path to take may not always be clear, particularly as they are known for being multitalented. Whilst a career choice may be undecided, belonging to the second house in the zodiac calendar representing wealth will mean that dreams of money and fortune will no doubt be a driving force for all Taureans. A career in finance, such as investment banking, could be a satisfying job, as they will enjoy watching their investments grow over time. High-risk decisions won't be appealing to Taureans. Rather, a steadfast investment is something that will likely attract them to parting with their hard-earned money.

Whilst Taureans may be naturally good at a job in finance, the more negative characteristics associated with this sign, such as greed and being overly materialistic, may mean that this avenue is best avoided to help keep these traits at bay. A more grounded career, influenced by this sign's earth element, may be complementary to a happy work life. The gradual and sustainable process of growing plants or vegetables lends itself to the slow-paced Taurean, so perhaps a career in horticulture would be well suited. Taureans' appreciation of beauty may lead to work in conservation, appealing to their nurturing side and their love of Mother Earth. Whether it is through full-time work or a leisurely activity, being in nature will have a positive and calming effect, and offer balance and perspective.

Ruled by Venus, the planet of beauty, the sign of Taurus has great potential for pursuing a career in the arts. Some of the best-known artists, including Salvador Dalí and William Shakespeare, are Taureans. Taureans strongly value security, and might struggle with the uncertainty of success, financial or otherwise, that a life in the arts can offer. This dislike for unsteady work and working for no immediate money are things that arty Taureans will need to overcome. However, their determination to hone their craft by stubbornly working towards their goals day by day can mean the bright lights of fame and success will be the ultimate pay-off. Taureans are known for not just appreciating beauty but also for being beautiful themselves, so perhaps a career in acting or fashion, like Taurean supermodel Gigi Hadid, may prove fulfilling.

As with family, colleagues cannot be chosen. Therefore, it can be advantageous to use star signs to learn about their key characteristics and discover the best ways of working together. As co-workers, Leonians can have a positive influence on Taureans by encouraging them to make bolder choices. However, Taureans may find Leonians difficult bosses, as neither the Bull nor the Lion is likely to admit defeat graciously. Taureans are multitalented in the workplace, and share many skills with other signs; from their problem-solving initiative that links them with practical Virgoans, to the resolute ambition they share with desirous Scorpians. These appealing attributes, together with their calm and patient nature, make Taureans liked and valued by their colleagues.

HEALTH AND WELLBEING

· · · · · · · · · · · · · · · · · · ·

Being a lover of the finest food and drink, Taureans can sometimes struggle with keeping their weight down. Not ones to deny themselves the luxury of eating out at fine restaurants, those calories can add up as high as their bill. And what's dinner without dessert? By making more meals from scratch at home, Taureans will be more aware of the ingredients going into their favourite foods. Taureans are known for their pre-planning and organisation skills. By utilising these positive traits in the kitchen, Taureans can prepare healthy meals ahead of time, and ensure that they are eating a more balanced diet.

Taurus rules the throat and neck and, like the Bull, it is often a Taurean's strongest area. Perhaps that is why this sign is known for being home to some of the most famous singers of all time, from James Brown to Ella Fitzgerald and Adele. Even if a Taurean does not enjoy singing, it may be beneficial to take extra care of this area by always wearing a scarf in the colder months and avoiding drinking too much alcohol that could aggravate the throat.

Bulls are strong with a stocky build, and Taureans often find success in weightlifting or gymnastics. However, earth is the element that guides Taurus and so physical exercise is likely to be enjoyed more so in Mother Nature than it is in the confines of a man-made gym. Walking is a wonderful form of regular and gentle exercise that Taureans can enjoy at an adjustable speed that is comfortable for them. Not only will walking or running outdoors help with maintaining a level of physical health, it will also make sure that they stay connected to nature where they feel their calmest.

Maintaining a healthy mind is just as important as listening to what the body needs. Taureans can be stubborn and unforgiving of people that they feel have wronged them. If fixated on, this negativity can be extremely harmful for Taureans and may even manifest itself in physical pain, such as a tight neck and shoulders. By practising forgiveness and letting go of negative emotions, Taureans should find that they are much happier and healthier, and are able to refocus on what brings them joy. Exercise that centres on bringing balance to the mind as well as the body, such as yoga or t'ai chi, will help calm the aggravated Bull.

Jealousy can also be another internal sore sport for any Taurean. Whilst it is a normal emotion experienced by most, Taureans can feel its sting too often in their relationships, and it may become a real cause of pain if left to fester. By questioning why these feelings of jealousy arise, Taureans can then work towards nipping those negative emotions in the bud.

Taurus

....

DAILY FORECASTS
for 2022

OCTOBER
. . . .

Saturday 1st

The planetary energy is pretty heavy today. What begins as a day with unhelpful restrictions becomes a day when you wish you had never got up. You can't do anything right today. Spend quality time at home with a few good travel documentaries and mentally plan your next trip.

Sunday 2nd

Mercury turns direct today and, as if by magic, you may see mists fall away to reveal a truth that has been hidden. This may be within your love life or your friendship circle. You may have a heavy heart as you take baby steps to process what this means for you.

Monday 3rd

Draw on useful skills you learned in the past and use them again. If added to your current workload, they may make you more efficient and productive. You could realise the value of going slowly with certain projects and apply these old skills in a truly innovative way.

Tuesday 4th

As the energy shifts, you seek more connection with others. That may be business meetings or social networking with like-minded people. You may meet someone new who can support any inner work you now need to do. However, scrutinise them and check their credentials. Then give them a fair chance.

Wednesday 5th

It may take you all day to pick up the pace. The problem is that you may feel stuck and reluctant to move in the wrong way. You may have to take a leap of faith and running right into a boundary problem. Mental activity is high but confusing.

Thursday 6th

Today, your interest groups may provide the stimulation you need. It may feel a little like you're swimming alone in a big ocean until you meet up with your circle. This can provoke emotions from deep inside, which can surface and have you asking big questions such as, "where do I belong?"

Friday 7th

Good grounding energy gives you a life jacket to help you keep afloat. You may get too used to this ethereal energy and drift far away, but your inner voice tells you to go back to the shore. Once there, you may do some rational and practical thinking, which suits you.

Saturday 8th

You catch sight of your true north, your inner compass. This may be your saving grace today, which pulls you back to the earthly plane. If you have a muddled mind, go with your heart. This evening you are more inspired to think about what needs to be put right.

Sunday 9th

Pluto turns direct and leads you to a full moon, which lights up the darkest corners of your psyche. You could have a startling realisation of what needs to change. You may let go of something you have been holding on to for too long. This might include a romance.

Monday 10th

Schedule a health check-up and get in touch with people you have neglected recently. Decisions regarding your resources may be made easier today if you take time to process what you need and what has been holding you back. End the day by doing something you love.

Tuesday 11th

Negotiations around your mundane duties could begin now. You may be considering dropping some of your responsibilities or delegating them elsewhere. If this can be done, you might see a glimpse of a future life with more time to choose what and who you spend time with.

Wednesday 12th

Your emotions are centred around how you appear to others. This may cause you to aim for making big impacts on important people. It could be that you step outside the box and take on a role which is new and exciting. If it aligns with your personal truth, go for it.

Thursday 13th

Money and possessions may be a theme today. You might need to do some networking or learn a new skill to help you manage this. Put your mind to this and you will master it in no time. It may be a juggling act to make things fair.

Friday 14th

Plenty of air energy continues to help you with mental tasks. You could be doing a job for the greater good and getting a lot of satisfaction from it. Your ruler, Venus, is giving you some tips about how beautiful harmony and equilibrium can be. She may also bring in the money today.

Saturday 15th

Today you are driven to connect with family members and share the love. You may feel protective of the young or wish to be mothered yourself. Make sure that whatever you choose doesn't conflict with others and cause a few triggers to go off. Childhood habits and wounds could reappear.

Sunday 16th

You may desire a familial connection or need meaningful, nurturing conversations. However, this might become cumbersome as you may be coerced into taking on more responsibilities. There may be some guilt involved, but stay strong and say no if others are asking too much. Remember, you are trying to lighten your load.

Monday 17th

It's possible that you experience passive-aggressive behaviour now. Family members or people you deal with in close relationships may be manipulative and demand more of your time and energy than you are comfortable giving. This could be part of your lessons this year. Perfect the art of give and take in relationships.

Tuesday 18th

Speak your truth and stand up for yourself today. You may need to roar louder than usual. Fiery energy helps you to be assertive and make sure that your own needs are met. Be careful that this doesn't lead to hot tempers and harsh words which can't be retracted.

Wednesday 19th

Another challenging day may begin with your good intentions to keep the peace. However, you might bump up against a few restrictions or roadblocks and wish you hadn't bothered. You or someone else could be pretty stubborn, and unless someone backs down, this won't be resolved any time today.

Thursday 20th

As your mood lifts, you might wish to try a different approach to achieving peace. Family members have been able to support you and are now encouraging you to be bold. This may mean that an apology is in order. Accept one or make one.

Friday 21st

This might be a good time to look at your finances. It may be that you have old subscriptions to be renewed or cancelled. You could also have funds invested with another person that need reviewing. Clean up your bank balance and get creative with new money-making ideas.

Saturday 22nd

You may have some ingenious ideas today which you are keen to implement. These might not involve your vision plan or true north. They could, however, include a romantic relationship or a creative project. A switch-up or declutter of your working space will make room for new, exciting things.

Sunday 23rd

It's important to check in with your health and your important relationships now. There may be something you have neglected to do which needs urgent attention. Saturn turns direct and lifts restrictions in the workplace. Prepare for some intense partner time as both Venus and the Sun enter your relationship zone.

Monday 24th

Your head and heart are in sync and you can give yourself a good talking to. It's likely that you are reconciling something to yourself or trying to justify some recent action. You can begin the working week with your head held high and a resolution to be responsible.

Tuesday 25th

A new moon and solar eclipse in your relationship area can help you set intentions which may take you to uncharted waters. This could be an intensely romantic time as Venus is in the mix.

Wednesday 26th

Thoughts of past relationships or difficult times may surface. You may try to stuff them back inside, but they continue to play on your mind. They have the potential to throw you right off track, so you need to face them head-on and deal with them respectfully and responsibly.

Thursday 27th

You may have a sleepless night as your mind is wandering and uncontrollable. Try to consider problems from different angles. Illusions and confusion confound you. Wait until you have some clarity. A burst of energy this afternoon may distract you from your worries. Take care and use it wisely.

Friday 28th

Today you may be more outgoing and willing to connect with friends or associates. Supportive groups may be somewhere for you to hide out for the weekend. You could find a guru or leader who can walk and talk you through any psychological issues that keep repeating themselves.

Saturday 29th

Merging and being part of a team or group feels right for you now. You may be able to communicate something you've been struggling with. Reach out to people who are empathic and are familiar with dealing with emotions. You may make deep conversation with a lover this evening.

Sunday 30th

Mars turns retrograde today. This may slow you down and dampen your enthusiasm. Try not to push or move against the flow during this time. Other energy suggests you are outgoing and cheerful. You may have had a weight lifted from your mind and feel at peace.

Monday 31st

Something is ready to be changed or let go of. Close the
door on that particular episode. This may have been a long,
hard climb, but you will soon see the benefits of doing your
inner work.

NOVEMBER

· · · · · · · · · · · · · · · · · ·

Tuesday 1st

You may have a difficult day at work. This could bring out the worst in you and people see a side that you would rather keep hidden in your professional life. Your stubborn side may not budge, and you could be unwilling to work well with others. Keep a level head and don't lose your cool.

Wednesday 2nd

Mars hits you with a roadblock and tries to teach you to be more flexible. There are ways around this, but you may need someone to point them out. You might desire to switch off and shut out the world. Problems in your love life may remind you of the past.

Thursday 3rd

You may find that your emotions are being filtered through a different lens. The ability to investigate your own deep truths might bring you to an understanding of why you relate as you do. If you have some revelations today, be prepared to take on the advice.

Friday 4th

Your inner compass is in front of you but may be hazy and confusing. Does it still hold value for you? Are you still aligned? You may have a period of adjustment to go through which you feel slows you down. Emotions may be too big to deal with sensibly today.

Saturday 5th

Drop down into your private thoughts and investigate a few old habits. Your conditioned behaviour may be preventing your growth. Try to learn new ways of responding that are more beneficial to you. This could shake up the dust of old relationships and affect a current one.

Sunday 6th

You could feel the benefit of taking things slowly today. This is your usual default, but if you're told to slow down, you usually do the opposite. Try not to resist a change or ending this evening. Ghosts from the past whisper in your ear and you may need to exorcise them.

Monday 7th

Put your best foot forward today and rejoin society. Problems in relating may affect the quality of your work. Do your best to get your duties and obligations done before attempting to right any wrongs with a partner. If you want it, do all it takes to get it.

Tuesday 8th

A full moon and lunar eclipse in your sign may close a window on love, money and other heavy issues. This wild card energy may make you unstable and restless today. Say nothing. Listen to and observe what is going on around you.

Wednesday 9th

Be very careful what you say today. You might upset someone, probably a partner. This may stir up some old troubles. You could get a good look at how some of your habits have been preventing you from living the life you want.

Thursday 10th

Setting boundaries or making agreements within relationships may be needed. This won't be easy, but the window is open for you to at least express your thoughts on this. You may be conflicted about what you want from a partner and how that fits in with your life purpose. Work on this now.

Friday 11th

Look at the things or concepts that hold value for you. Are you filling your life up with material things that hold no meaningful connection? You may enjoy your luxuries and special objects, but if real love connection is what you seek, you won't find it within them.

Saturday 12th

Emotions can be strong or overwhelming today. Conversations or trips to family may lead you to spill more of your truth than you would normally. If family are your safety net, then this is fine. Right now, you wish to be nurtured and loved as if you were a child again.

Sunday 13th

Helpful planetary energy is available for you to set a few things straight. Try not to be sucked into fantastical or wishful thinking. Love and harmony, when accepted, can make a big difference to you. Be prepared to trawl the depths of your psyche and let go of old stuff.

Monday 14th

Grieving for something you have lost, has expired or is outdated is fine. Honour that it had a presence in your life. You may be more able to open up and speak from the heart now. Make sure that it's honest, kind and respectful. You have more courage today to do this.

Tuesday 15th

Things are changing, and you may need to have an important talk to a lover today. This may be a turning point and you will need to pause and carefully consider your options before proceeding. If you feel stuck, listen to your feelings and that inner voice. Don't use power to provoke.

Wednesday 16th

If you take your time and remain open and honest, you could see your relationship deepening. Communication is the key here, especially letting your partner in on what your dreams and visions are. They may come on board with you or they may not, but they will be supportive.

Thursday 17th

You may be in the mood to discover things that are mysterious, foreign or appeal to your sensuous side. If learning new subjects or languages is your thing, now is a good time. Cultures and philosophies might be a trigger point for travel and make your world a bit bigger.

. . . .

Friday 18th

This may simply be a day where you get on with your work and ignore outside distractions. This evening you could feel them calling, but know that it isn't the right time to act. You might be irritated by this, but you can do the things which call later.

Saturday 19th

Do your weekend duties and meet your obligations. You may leave space to dream and play later on. A feeling of satisfaction can fill you with pride, knowing that you've had a well-balanced day. Intimacy and deep love await you this evening. Make the most of it.

Sunday 20th

Mental stimulation may be what you need today. Someone could call upon you to fix a problem or act as an authority figure. Your opinions and advice might be sought after. It's also possible that you're negotiating a deal which will enhance your career. Be someone to look up to now.

Monday 21st

This is an interesting time for love. As the Sun leaves this area, the moon enters. This may mean that fears or worries surface. However, if the groundwork has been done with the Sun, this won't be a problem. Deep emotional bonding gives you the freedom to talk tonight.

Tuesday 22nd

There is a trigger which keeps coming up and is now screaming for your attention. This has to do with past relationships or times when you had intense feelings or fears. Thinking about this today may cause some tremors inside you and threaten to shift your mood to a negative one.

Wednesday 23rd

Your feelings may be turbulent as you navigate your way through old territory. There's no use in digging up the old unless you intend to dispose of it altogether. Make it into a ritual. Honour the place it once held in your life and let it go with love.

Thursday 24th

Hold out your arms for the many blessings you're about to receive today. Jupiter turns direct and a new moon signals a new and intimate journey. Venus and Mercury are involved too, so discuss what you desire with your partner, pack up and hit the road together.

Friday 25th

There's no need to rush today. You may be trying to attach to your inner compass, but it's evading you. Just enjoy the breath of fresh air and stop pushing against the flow. This evening you might see that your efforts were futile and resolve to be sensible at the next attempt.

Saturday 26th

It's a good weekend to plan effectively for the months to come. You may be itching to travel now, especially with a partner. Use this time to research and make a vision board of what you wish to explore. Broaden your horizons on many different levels and enjoy yourself.

Sunday 27th

Think of the most improbable things you'd like to do and then plan for them. It may be time to break the mould and go beyond your comfort zone. Just be realistic. You might feel completely in control of your life right now and can set about making big ideas.

Monday 28th

You can be fiercely outgoing today. This is great and fills you with optimism, but Mars is asking you to think twice, make sure you are clear and think again. You may come up against a hurdle if you haven't covered all the options. Pause and assess everything in your game plan now.

Tuesday 29th

Your mind may be doing overtime and not letting you rest. Keep your mind on your work or your distractions will be noticed by an authority figure. A course of higher education may fill the gap you have until you can get away and experience things for yourself.

Wednesday 30th

It's possible that your enthusiasm is infecting others in the workplace and your wider circles. If you can pitch some ideas to the boss, you may be able to combine travel with work. You may be getting a spiritual high at this time, which helps you put a few things in perspective.

DECEMBER

· · · · · · · · · · · · · · · · · ·

Thursday 1st

Tread lightly today, the energy suggests you could be easily upset by friends, social groups or lovers. Check finances or investments you have with another person. There may be some disagreements about the value of these now. Be flexible and open to new ideas for managing money.

Friday 2nd

Your empathy may be limitless today, but this can make you tired and you could need alone time. Conversations with a lover could be difficult or border on the taboo. You may wish to consider whether this is in line with your personal truths and inner compass. Remember your own boundaries.

Saturday 3rd

You may be passionate today and wish to see some action. This could involve some deep investigations into your psyche or a deep desire to be intimate with a lover. However, with Mars retrograde, you might find that your own home is the best place to be right now.

Sunday 4th

Neptune turns direct. Using your inner compass, review what you have noticed in past months. Have illusions faded away? Have you taken off the rose-coloured spectacles? You may have a crisis of conscience now and realise that something you have invested deeply in is not as it once seemed.

Monday 5th

Today you may have an overwhelming desire for truth. It's possible that you feel that you've wasted time and no longer know what is right for you. This energy will pass, so don't dwell on it too much. Look to the future and start shaking things up. Find your inner rebel.

Tuesday 6th

Conversations may reveal a truth or deception. You might be shocked at first, but when you have had time to process it, you may be relieved. All eyes are on you, so ensure that your responses are adult and responsible. Take stock of what brings you joy and quality now.

Wednesday 7th

Take time to gather your thoughts and be at peace with yourself. If your mind wanders, let it. Try not to fixate on one thing as you may reverse your thinking in the future. Learning about what you value is an important lesson as it also teaches you what you don't want.

Thursday 8th

Today's full moon may spotlight exactly what you treasure and need around you. As Mars is also there, you may feel irritable or find it hard to accept some losses. Put your mind to your work and do your tasks. Practical and mental activities will distract from your emotions.

Friday 9th

Putting up your defences may not be a good idea now. Instead, try being vulnerable and allowing close relatives, especially maternal types to comfort you. Good home-cooked food and familiar habits are needed now. Nourish your soul and let others care for you. Get into your safety zone.

Saturday 10th

You may have a yearning to start something different now. A course of higher education may attract you. Travel could be on your mind. Choose something in which you can go at your own pace. The wider world is waiting for you. Make a plan.

Sunday 11th

Change may be difficult today, so make it small. It could simply be that you leave the company of a carer or close friend for now. Emotional energy is carrying you along and you may not be comfortable with this. By evening, you could find your voice and make it count.

Monday 12th

You have a good sense of duty and responsibility today and this will be noticed by those above you. Challenges may present themselves this evening as you might be recalling past loves and intimate moments. These must stay in the past as they aren't going to help you now.

Tuesday 13th

Being stubborn and wanting your own way is not a good look. You may be fighting anyone who crosses your path today and coming across as childish or defiant. Use that fiery energy to do something productive. Get out the maps and think about a dream holiday to plan.

Wednesday 14th

Grounding energy gives you some relief today. You're at your best when doing practical activity. Try getting creative or decluttering a messy area. This could also be a time to detox your body ready for the heavy festive season. Be good to yourself today and get some quality self-care.

Thursday 15th

The good energy continues to keep you occupied with worthwhile pursuits. If you experience a sudden blockage or tiredness, don't stress about it. It will resolve itself this afternoon and the breakthrough may give you a great deal of satisfaction. You could even rebel a little or invent something. Congratulate or reward yourself.

Friday 16th

There may be no time for dreaming today as your inner compass evades you. Perhaps there is too much to do and your mundane duties are piling up. This may get you down a little, but these are necessary jobs and need to be done. Deadlines may be calling you.

Saturday 17th

Balance will not be easily achieved today. You may need to delegate some jobs or ask for help. Weekend fun may come, but there might be a lot to do first. When it does, let your hair down and have fun. You may be outrageous today at an early festive party.

Sunday 18th

This may be another day where you are needed to make preparations or just show up and say your piece. There may be decisions where your opinion is valued. If this interferes with your free time you may need to sit tight, get on with it and do your duty.

Monday 19th

Love is on the agenda today as your special relationships are harmonic and pleasing. You may get something now that you have been yearning for recently. Shared dreams and passions make it easier for you to relate to a partner. Maybe you are planning a trip together.

Tuesday 20th

A little loving can go a long way today. Mutual respect and joy with a partner can provide you with a sense of inner peace. The future looks brighter and you are ready to begin the journey towards it. You may have matured in a relationship or the relationship itself has evolved.

Wednesday 21st

The winter solstice arrives to lead you into the darker nights. Choose to use this day to pause, reflect and give gratitude for the year gone by. It suits you to schedule some activities that take you deeper into yourself and others that explore the wider world.

Thursday 22nd

As the festive days approach quickly, you may find you are more tired than usual. It would help if you aimed to co-operate and not make your own agenda. You may wish to switch up the normal or traditional ways of doing things. Be respectful to all you share this time with.

Friday 23rd

A new moon is a great opportunity to make plans for things that have several steps and may take a long time to achieve. Slowly suits you, as you're aware. You may be asked to take a leadership role now or in the New Year. Consider if this aligns with your journey.

Saturday 24th

This is a great day for conversations that reach out to touch the heart of another. It's an emotional day but filled with promise and hope for a bright future. Your inner rebel is itching to come out and this may just be the party animal getting ready.

Sunday 25th

Self-control is important today. You may be hosting the celebrations, but if you aren't, you need to let another shine. You could be more altruistic than usual and may enjoy the peace this gives you deep inside. A heart filled with optimism is a heart worth sharing with others.

Monday 26th

Today may present small challenges and will almost certainly be about relating to others. You might need more time alone, but your obligations prevent this. Try not to show any resentment and play your role in the family today. Remember personal boundaries and remain respectful. Pitch in and do your bit.

Tuesday 27th

Friends and social groups have your attention now. Perhaps an escape is needed. Your empathy is strong, and you may wish to merge with like-minded folk either online or in your community. Ethereal energy helps you to be hopeful, flexible and part of a loving circle.

Wednesday 28th

You may be in exactly the right frame of mind to connect to your inner compass. There is a good chance that you feel more connected now than all year. Your dreams and intentions seem aligned and ready for you to approach. Start that journey now and remember this feeling.

Thursday 29th

Mercury turns retrograde to see the year out. You may need to be more adaptable now. Remember to back up devices and make communication crystal clear. Love talk may experience misunderstanding today, but if you're aware of Mercury's tricks, you can be more meticulous when speaking, planning and travelling.

Friday 30th

The holiday season may have worn you out and today you feel its effects. To save your energy for another party, take a day to yourself or on the sofa with favourite movies. Don't commit to visitors if you don't have the energy. If you do, you may get irritable.

Saturday 31st

Challenging energy ends the year and you may not be in the mood to celebrate. You could be feeling manipulated or coerced into something you're unsure of. You may even feel trapped by the confines of family and friends or have had enough of partying. Do the right thing and retreat if you're overwhelmed.

Taurus

....

DAILY FORECASTS
for 2023

JANUARY

. . . .

Sunday 1st

New Year's Day is traditionally the time to set new resolutions.
Before doing so, however, it's worth considering what you're
ready to let go of. Make a concerted effort to shed toxic energy
and release any resentments or negativity. Wipe the slate clean
as a new year begins.

Monday 2nd

You may be reminiscing with a dear friend today. This might
be someone you met when you were travelling or studying.
Turn your attention towards the past by going through old
photos and remembering happy times. This could act as a
trigger for your next big adventure.

Tuesday 3rd

Turn your attention towards work and money. When it comes
to career or vocational success, it's not what you know but who
you know that can help you make swift progress. This is a good
time to initiate new projects and ideas and use technology to
good effect.

Wednesday 4th

Look out for someone who can help you achieve what you
want: a role model, business partner or joint venture. This is a
positive period for a work-related partnership. Get on the right
side of someone in a position of power and it can make a big
difference to your reputation.

Thursday 5th

There may be a foreign or global theme in your life now, whether you're keen to be an activist or volunteer, helping others and fulfilling a mission in the process. Your astrology is calling you off the couch, asking you to engage with your next steps, where you're heading and why.

Friday 6th

Today's full moon is ideal for expanding your horizons. You may be considering a course of study, be thinking about your beliefs or have a desire to emigrate or move abroad. You could be acutely aware today of what's possible and what's not when you get real about your situation.

Saturday 7th

When Mercury's retrograde, your attention turns towards the past. This might be a time when you're reconnecting with people you met in a previous life, or you're remembering a time when you were a free spirit and you travelled the world and put freedom before security.

Sunday 8th

Keep dreaming and don't give up on your future goals. This is a positive time of year for you to visualise what you want and make your dreams happen. Turning points will come later this month. For now, write a cosmic wish list and take steps to turn your ideas into reality.

Monday 9th

Put your faith in another person today. If they promised
you a pay rise or you're waiting on a payment, this is likely
to materialise before too long. It could be paperwork that's
holding you up or a bureaucratic delay over the holiday period.
Double-check everything.

Tuesday 10th

You may be in the process of stepping down from a position of
leadership or responsibility. If you've been in a specific role for
the last two years, you're probably right. Make your intentions
known as a new wave of leadership could begin soon.

Wednesday 11th

It's a good day to review travel or study plans. Wait before
booking a holiday or course until Mercury turns direct next
week. For now, do your research and ensure you have all
the information you need to get moving. This may include
checking out visas and entry requirements.

Thursday 12th

2023 is not a year to play small by any means. What takes
place this week could help you see where progress can be
made. This is not only about your work and vocation but also
finances and where you invest your time and energy. Chase up
a payment or outstanding debt.

Friday 13th

There's nothing suspicious about this Friday 13th. Focus your
attention on earnings and career progress and you have a great
chance to do well. If money was held up for whatever reason
over the last couple of months, you now have a green light to
improve your finances.

Saturday 14th

You may be on a roll with work and want to spend the weekend getting ahead. Be wary of doing so, however, and know that giving yourself a complete break would be preferable. It's a good weekend to look after yourself and take precious care of your mind, body and spirit.

Sunday 15th

You may be feeling out of sorts today. Perhaps you didn't sleep well last night or you're finding it hard to settle to any activity. If you're feeling impulsive or jangly about your work or career, it's not the time to act. If your emotions are all over the place, wait until you feel calmer.

Monday 16th

A close relationship promises both passion and intensity, yet experiencing strong emotions could leave you feeling unsettled. If you're finding it hard to concentrate at work, you may need to take a step back from love for now or detach yourself from a personal issue.

Tuesday 17th

Business and pleasure don't mix now, so ensure you keep the two separate. A heart-to-heart with a loved one first thing could help to settle your emotions. If you're looking for new ideas on how to fund a travel or study project, think big this evening and draw up some plans.

Wednesday 18th

Mercury turns direct in your travel and study zone today, which means it's a good time to review these areas of your life. There may be significant changes to your plans. Or, you might be ready to commit to plans that were made earlier this year. Dig deep and make your move.

Thursday 19th

Turn your attention towards joint finances and shared resources. Look at ways you can free up your money to invest in your future or new experiences. It may feel daunting to take a big financial step but if it helps you create the life you want for yourself, go for it.

Friday 20th

It's all going on at the peak of your horoscope from today as the Sun enters your career and vocation zone. This is great news for your ambitious side. Whether you're applying for a new job, a promotion, or you're full of ideas, it's go-for-it time.

Saturday 21st

You have a strong opportunity to crack on with what you want for yourself and your career or vocational goals. Be innovative, consider new trends, update your website and keep moving forwards. The new moon in Aquarius turns a spotlight to the future and all things new.

Sunday 22nd

Your current astrology signals a time of adventure when you're ready to stretch your comfort zone and do things differently. You might make a major decision this weekend that impacts your future life. Use modern technology and new trends to expand your online network.

Monday 23rd

It would be easy to go it alone now, yet this might prove exhausting in the long run, so work at your relationships, both personal and professional. Keep your emotions out of the equation. Instead, use logic and rationality if you're making a big work decision.

Tuesday 24th

Don't lose sight of the social side of life. The focus has been on work and future goals for some time, but you'll be happier with a healthy work/life balance. Talking to friends about a holiday or travel plans could get you revved up about booking a spontaneous trip away.

Wednesday 25th

Ensure you have good friends in your life who inspire you and encourage you to further your dreams. When you're in tune with a friend, the two of you can conjure up some mutual hopes and wishes. Caring and compassion ebb and flow between you and the ones you love.

Thursday 26th

Other people are going to play a significant role in your life from this week onwards. Yet it's still important that you spend some time on your own, especially if you have a big decision to make. Tap into the spiritual side of life today and listen to your inner guidance.

Friday 27th

Venus's change of star sign today helps for connecting with friends or teaming up with someone close to explore all things new and different. You might want to back out of a social event or a date, but it's worth making an extra effort to reach out and connect.

Saturday 28th

The moon is in your star sign. This is a safe harbour that means it's an ideal day to line up activities that are comforting and nurturing. You could choose to be in the bosom of your family or have an indulgent time with friends. Do what's right for you.

Sunday 29th

Be spontaneous today and ring the changes. If you're typical of your star sign, you can be resistant to change, but your current astrology is encouraging you to try an alternative path. Your use of technology could be revelatory and you may find yourself ahead of the pack.

Monday 30th

It's a fast-paced start to the working week. Make the most of dynamic energy in your work and money zones and get things moving fast. If you need to be more competitive, go for it. If you can sense your ambition rising, tap into your drive and determination.

. . . .

Tuesday 31st

If you've not already booked that trip away or a new course
of study, there's still time. Don't wait too long or you might
talk yourself out of it. Spontaneous moves are recommended.
When it comes to money, be assertive and ensure you're paid
what you deserve.

FEBRUARY

Wednesday 1st

Pay more attention to the practical side of life today. Consider your resources and do what you can to ensure you're safe and secure. As one of the earth signs, you're at your best when you have strong foundations in your life. Work on the basics so you feel more grounded.

Thursday 2nd

If you've lost faith recently, it's a good day to offer up a prayer. Alternatively, spend time with people who know how to nurture and care for you. There's no big rush today. Instead, savour the small moments of wonder and make time for neighbours and your local community.

Friday 3rd

Watch your rebel tendencies. Some people think of you as being calm and collected, but you're not the Bull of the zodiac for no reason. Try to be a team player at work rather than being overly dogmatic or stubborn. Going out on a limb is a daring move.

Saturday 4th

You and your partner may not see eye-to-eye, whether the issue is a friendship or money disagreement. It would be a good weekend to get together with family or have a celebration at home. Take some time out now, especially if work is keeping you busy.

Sunday 5th

It's a good weekend to make an intuitive decision as the light of the full moon brings clarity and insight. You may be reassessing the work/life balance and realise that your presence is required more at home. Don't give up on your goals but keep your personal life healthy too.

Monday 6th

If there's someone in your family who disapproves of what you're doing, this may be more evident today. Be aware of your differences and don't think that you have to win them over. At the same time, don't give up on your future goals, especially those involving travel or study.

Tuesday 7th

You gravitate towards creative activities over the next couple of days. You may be catching up with a hobby or be improving a skill or talent. As long as you don't overspend, this is a positive way to express your feelings and be true to who you are.

Wednesday 8th

A strong part of you may want to pull back from your duties today. There's an indulgent feel to your stars and you may be more interested in romance, children and good times. Love and friendship are linked and a friend might declare their affections, or perhaps you're on a first date.

Thursday 9th

Keep a sense of balance today and aim for more peace and harmony in your surroundings. It doesn't matter whether you're at work or home, you'll benefit from being in a calmer environment. Take good care of your health now and prioritise your fitness levels or exercise routine.

Friday 10th

It may feel as if it's now or never for a travel or study opportunity. Whatever's been bubbling away since December 2022, there's some truth in this. It might not be long before your career or vocation kicks into a new gear. Either be decisive and go or cancel that holiday.

Saturday 11th

Use this weekend to focus on the future and what's next in your life. When the personal planets move across the peak of your horoscope, this lights up your public persona, how other people see you and getting ahead in the world. A conversation could reawaken your ambition.

Sunday 12th

Don't forget the ones you love. You might be so busy getting excited about the future that you ignore your partner or loved ones. Ideally, involve your other half with your plans rather than go it alone. It is true, however, that this is your time and you may already know that.

Monday 13th

Reach out to someone special whether you arrange a lunchtime meet up or you send them a gift or romantic text. Love is in the ascendancy and you may be aware that your feelings are growing for someone close. Put love first today and you're in tune with your stars.

Tuesday 14th

A strong feeling of purpose can be energising today. You may be aware of another person's influence in your life and recognise your true self in the process. The more you give to others, the more you receive in return. Be open to the flow of love and abundance.

Wednesday 15th

You may be experiencing moments of bliss in your life. Your planet Venus is in the part of your horoscope that can awaken romance, your creative source or spiritual transcendence. Trust your emotions and give in to them completely. Spend time with your friends later on.

Thursday 16th

You may need to set some clear boundaries at work or with a person in a position of authority. If you're under pressure, try to hand over some of your responsibilities. If you're unemployed or dislike your job, explore a new avenue of work.

Friday 17th

Diligence and hard work are the order of the day. Complete what you've started and aim to finish a work deadline this weekend. If you're typical of your star sign, you know that significant change requires effort and a long-term plan. Keep your eye on your future goals.

Saturday 18th

You may spend some of this weekend dealing with work or responsibilities. If this is so, do make time for friendship and socialising as well to keep a healthy balance. The Sun's move into Pisces highlights your friendships and group activities. It's time to expand your social life.

Sunday 19th

Think carefully about who you spend time with and notice how much you're enjoying yourself. Today is the dark side of the moon and traditionally a time for rest and retreat. It's also ideal for reassessing your friendships and noticing who you want to hang out with more.

Monday 20th

Today's new moon promises new beginnings. It may present you with an ideal opportunity to join a new group, club or society. This period is especially strong for networking and making the right kind of connections that can help boost your profile and reputation. Reach out to other people.

Tuesday 21st

If you're experiencing a pull in different directions, don't take on too much. It is important now and over the next few weeks that you prioritise your spiritual life and inner work. Think of this as a chance to recharge your emotional energy. Learn to say no as well as yes.

Wednesday 22nd

Pace yourself today and be clever in using your time well. Gravitate towards activities that leave you feeling renewed and refreshed. One conversation could help you make swift progress with a work or money issue. Act fast this evening and you could line up a promising opportunity.

Thursday 23rd

Find time to prioritise your inner world as this will make a big difference to your confidence levels. When you feel good about yourself, this automatically has a knock-on effect in the workplace or regarding a job application or interview. Be determined to get what you want.

Friday 24th

It would be a good day to line up a breakfast meeting or aim to get into work earlier than usual. Start as you mean to go on and you're more likely to have a productive end to the working week. This evening is ideal to meet up with friends at one of your favourite venues.

Saturday 25th

The moon is in Taurus for most of this weekend, which means you're wise to prioritise your needs over others'. You might change your schedule last minute if there's something urgent you want to attend to. It's not a day to follow the rules. Instead, go wherever your fancy takes you.

Sunday 26th

It's important to take a step back sometimes so you can see your progress out in the world from a different perspective. It's easy to get caught up on the hamster wheel of life, which leaves little time for working on your purpose or mission. Take a new look at the bigger picture.

. . . .

Monday 27th

The more you trust your capabilities and have faith that things will work out, the more you tune in to your good fortune. Luck is closely linked to your karma and past endeavours. Consider what this may mean for you. If you're seeking a private benefactor, follow up a lead today.

Tuesday 28th

Keep your eyes on the prize and don't give up on a money goal. Admittedly, your financial fortunes may have taken you on an unlikely diversion over the last six months but the end goal is in sight. Give yourself one more month to achieve what you set out to do.

MARCH
· · · · · · · · · · · · · · · · ·

Wednesday 1st

Your mental faculties are powered up today so make the most of this. It's an ideal day to get curious, come up with new ideas and find out key information. Communication in all its guises gets the green light, so write things down and have conversations. Reach out and connect.

Thursday 2nd

You may be ready to work less and play more. Life may step in to gift you, so you can do just that. Friendship is going to be an important theme in your life moving forwards. There could be a particular reason why. Perhaps you're simply ready to socialise more.

Friday 3rd

Your emotions could be extremely strong today. You may feel overly connected, whether you're sensitive to other people's opinions or today's news triggers an emotional response. Only spend time with a sibling or neighbour if you want to and don't put yourself under duress.

Saturday 4th

You may be sharing happy memories with your family today, or taking a trip down memory lane. It's all well and good having future goals in life, but it's important not to let go of the past completely. One of your previous connections could prove to be a godsend.

Sunday 5th

If there's something you want to discuss with a member of your family that impacts you both financially, today's the day. You could be talking about property prices or be thinking about getting a quote for household repairs. It's a good day for being proactive around the home.

Monday 6th

You may step into a position of leadership now. Perhaps you're ready to leap in and look after those in need. If a good friend calls on you this week, be there for them. It might be time for you to put your foot down and put firm boundaries in place.

Tuesday 7th

Today's full moon is about collaborating with other people rather than working solely on your own. This is where you can find success from delegating and teamwork, rather than trying to deal with everything by yourself. Be aware that a group of people may be relying on you.

Wednesday 8th

If you're worried about a child or lover, try not to let your emotions run away with you. Full moon energy can be exposing and you may need to consider how to handle a sensitive situation. Check out the reason for any reservations and notice where in life you're feeling fearful.

Thursday 9th

It would be easy now to escape into work, and you're indeed wise to do whatever helps you find equilibrium. You might be asking for a colleague's opinion on a personal issue, or just waiting a while to see what you think intuitively. There's no rush, take your time.

Friday 10th

Aim for a productive and peaceful day. Don't overcommit
yourself and agree to only deal with events and people that
trigger little or no stress in your life. This can be a hard call
but it will help you in more ways than one. Focus on the
things in your life that are tangible and practical.

Saturday 11th

If you know you need a night out, here's your opportunity.
Be spontaneous today and say yes to an invitation that comes
your way. Arrange something special with a new friend and
love could follow. Put work and personal issues to one side and
enjoy yourself wholeheartedly.

Sunday 12th

Your relationships are under the cosmic spotlight in a good
way. Being with someone you love or a person in your life who
gets who you are could help you find a new level of comfort.
Be open to loving connections, whether you're hanging out
with your friends or you're on a date.

Monday 13th

Turn your attention to money and joint finances today.
If there's something that's gone wrong financially or you're
waiting on a payment, sort things out or chase things up.
Don't let a non-payment add a black mark to your credit score.
Be persistent in your money-related deals.

Tuesday 14th

It would be easy now to let things slip and trust that everything's in order. Your hope and faith may feel strong, but not necessarily where the money's concerned. Take note of who you're dealing with and steer away from anyone slippery. Don't be fooled by a scam.

Wednesday 15th

You may feel disillusioned with a friendship group or club of which you're a member. It could be truly magical on the one hand or disorienting on the other hand. The best way to tap in to today's weird planetary vibe is to go with the flow and see where life leads you.

Thursday 16th

A group event could be spectacularly memorable. However, do be wary of lies and check in with your earthy common sense that you're not being lead astray. You might be easily persuaded now and it's wise not to be overly indulgent or headstrong. Keep your feet firmly on the ground.

Friday 17th

Venus in Taurus is sensual, affectionate, plentiful and abundant. Slow things down, savour life's pleasures and live in the moment. Rushing through life won't bring the fulfilment or satisfaction you crave. Instead, stop and notice the world around you. Hang out with beautiful people.

Saturday 18th

You may feel torn between work and socialising this weekend. You might have some catching up to do on the computer, or you may have been offered some overtime. Try and keep all aspects of your life balanced and don't give in entirely to work or play. Find a healthy compromise.

Sunday 19th

Mercury's move into Aries today highlights inner work and taking more time for yourself. If you're in a busy family situation or you've been spending a lot of time on the computer, it would be a good day to create some me time. Cancel a social event and chill out instead.

Monday 20th

Today is the equinox and the official start of spring. For you, this highlights kindness and caring and taps into the side of your nature that enjoys the slow life. Cook for others, take care of people, share love and be open to love. Practise the art of gratitude.

Tuesday 21st

This is a good time to trust your intuition as today's new moon turns your attention inwards. Create more space in your life so you have time to reflect and contemplate. When key planets are in Aries, the star sign before yours, think of this as a period of preparation and gestation.

Wednesday 22nd

You're looking at your life through fresh eyes, ready to let go of any projects that aren't working out or connections that sap your energy. This is a wonderful time to develop your spiritual path or find your faith, whether through religion or a connection with life beyond the individual.

Thursday 23rd

Today's astrology indicates a powerful transformation in your life that could be important for where you're heading and why. This might entail closing a door on the past or letting go of a job or position of status. Wherever in life you're ready to make a stand, here's your opportunity.

Friday 24th

Dive deep into simple pleasures. Walk in nature, produce and cook food, have a massage, slow down and indulge your creative or artistic talents. Also, be open to love and prioritise quality time with your partner. It's even more important to do so if you're shocked by recent events at work.

Saturday 25th

Action planet Mars is on the move today and lights up your communication sector. This is a cue to direct more energy into new friendships and make connections close to home. Catch up with a sibling or neighbour and find out what's happening in your local neighbourhood or community.

Sunday 26th

You may realise that you need to put some limitations on your spending. Consider your long-term goals and whether a savings plan would benefit you in the long run. Cutting out a small expense could make a big difference. Take a closer look at what you can do.

Monday 27th

It's all very well putting your faith in something and trusting that things will work out in the end. This is important to do but being one of the earth signs, you have a practical nature. Therefore, don't miss out on the planning or budgeting stage. Be cash savvy alongside being faithful.

Tuesday 28th

If you've lost faith or you're lacking in purpose, it's here where you need to inject some fresh energy. Think of this period as a time of renewal, rest and retreat. Then, you can enter your birthday month feeling refreshed, having cleared away the old to invite in the new.

Wednesday 29th

Make an effort to reach out to other people and make new connections in your life. You could find that someone you meet during this period becomes a life-long friend, so it's definitely worth it. If you want help or advice, turn to a neighbour, especially one who's older and wiser.

Thursday 30th

Your relationships could be lively today as your astrology
brings a thrill of excitement. This might be related to love or
serendipity or the luxurious side of life. What's important is
that you remain open to whoever or whatever comes your way.
The new connections theme remains strong.

Friday 31st

If you're at home or with your family today, you're in tune
with your stars. Being around the ones you love is where joy
and motivation can be found. You might be considering your
next home move or be encouraging someone younger to take
an independent step.

APRIL
· · · · · · · · · · · · · · · · ·

Saturday 1st

Make time for home and family. That might mean you have
to reschedule or change things around first thing. You'll feel
more settled in familiar surroundings where you can indulge
in whatever brings you comfort. Create time and space in your
life to relax and recharge your batteries.

Sunday 2nd

Love and romance could waft in today. However, there seems
to be a recurring block or obstacle. This could mean that
you're in love with a friend who's not interested in you.
Perhaps there's a repeat issue around children or commitment
that keeps rearing its head.

Monday 3rd

Communication planet Mercury enters Taurus, giving you
the gift of the gab. If you're feeling out of whack, as if you're
helping to boost someone else's success but not your own, this
could be the week to take stock and turn things around. Push
your agenda and don't give power to another.

Tuesday 4th

A new romance or love affair could be enjoyable but it may not
be easy if you don't know where you stand. As one of the earth
signs, you enjoy having strong foundations beneath your feet.
Look more closely at how a light-hearted relationship benefits
you and where it doesn't.

Wednesday 5th

Today's full moon could help you regain your balance and find a flow in your everyday lifestyle. Prioritise the things in life that make you happy and take care of yourself and others. Look for a new opportunity to reach out and connect, either at work or at the gym.

Thursday 6th

It would be easy to retreat now and hide away. Yet with the moon in social Libra, it feels more important to be in the world and create supportive alliances in your life. Teamwork can be a boon and can take some stress off your shoulders. Learn to delegate and ask for help.

Friday 7th

Turn your attention towards romantic relationships. Today is potentially passionate whether you're married or looking for love. It doesn't matter about your current situation as long as you're prepared to experience the magic of romance and to open your heart. Say yes to the lure of love.

Saturday 8th

Open the lines of communication today and initiate a first-step conversation or encounter. This may not be the only time you get together and try to work out an agreement or deal, yet what you put in place now is vital. Sow seeds and ask for what you want or need.

Sunday 9th

It may not be easy to address an issue around money, sex or a taboo topic. You may prefer to say nothing and hope that life steps in to sort things out. However, that's not the best approach. You may find it more challenging to speak up soon.

Monday 10th

Pay close attention to money and all forms of financial transactions. Whether you're talking about investments, an inheritance, savings or debt, a mortgage or loan, it's an excellent day to address money matters. Nothing is stopping you and there are lots of benefits to doing so.

Tuesday 11th

Venus enters Gemini and your money zone today, where it remains until May 7th. Gemini rules communication, so talk to people, fill out forms and be open and curious about what happens next. Read books to challenge your money mindset. Luck is an attitude so choose to be lucky.

Wednesday 12th

You may be talking about booking a holiday or trip away over the next couple of weeks. If so, you're in tune with your stars. Any time between April 21st to May 15th is ideal for taking a step back. Alternatively, sign up for a course of study.

Thursday 13th

You could be lacking confidence today, so don't try to run before you walk. Stop giving yourself a hard time if you feel unsure or unsettled and accept that you may be out of sorts. Focus on what you can achieve rather than aiming too high. Keep life simple.

Friday 14th

When it comes to money, don't think that you have to rush into anything new. It might be a better strategy to slow down and check what you're doing. If money's not forthcoming, try not to be disheartened. There will be other chances to boost your finances in the future.

Saturday 15th

You won't want to take work home with you this weekend unless you have to catch up. Mercury will turn retrograde in your star sign at the end of the coming week, so it's worth getting ahead before then. Deal with an application or prepare for a presentation.

Sunday 16th

If you want money advice, this isn't the best day to ask a friend. The same goes if you were hoping for a loan. What you could do is generate some new ideas yourself. It's a good day to be proactive and find out more about what's possible financially.

Monday 17th

Think of the coming week as a time of preparation rather than aiming to achieve a lot. Take the pace slow and be aware that you may experience more distractions or confusion than usual. A good friend could take up your time, and perhaps your emotional energy too.

Tuesday 18th

Take the pace slow and conserve your energy where possible. This is the dark of the moon and you may need more rest than usual. Avoid a discussion or debate if you know it's likely to end in an argument that could be time-consuming and potentially tiring too.

Wednesday 19th

If you're lacking confidence at the moment, practise being still and quiet. If you're religious, spend time in prayer. If you're on a spiritual path, try meditation or relaxation techniques. When you stop and listen, sometimes life offers you a gift that you wouldn't have discovered otherwise.

Thursday 20th

Today's solar eclipse takes place on the edge of your birthday month. Traditionally, a new moon represents new beginnings but this eclipse encourages you to consider what you're letting go. It could be an attitude or a belief.

Friday 21st

Your astrology feels intense. This could be the time when your stubborn nature kicks in, especially if you feel hard done by. Before over-reacting to a situation, know that Mercury turns retrograde today. Therefore, you're wise to let things be and review your options instead.

Saturday 22nd

Usually when the Sun enters Taurus, your confidence and energy levels rise. It's different this year, however, and you may be entering your birthday month under a certain amount of stress. If this is true for you, it's important to stop completely if you can, chill out and relax.

Sunday 23rd

Today's astrology is perfect for treating yourself and the ones you love. If it was a challenging end to the working week, you deserve to be treated well. And, if you're a typical Taurus, good food and wine, good friends and company can be all it takes to put the world to rights.

Monday 24th

You might return to a conversation or meeting that took place earlier this month. If so, this isn't the time to finalise matters. Instead, explore all your options. This could be related to a personal or professional issue. Go back to the drawing board and reconsider what comes next.

Tuesday 25th

It's a wonderful day to reconnect with old friends or get together with a group of people you used to hang out with a lot. This is one of the benefits of Mercury retrograde as it takes you back into the past and reminds you of happy memories. Reminisce over old times.

Wednesday 26th

Being with the people you know and trust will bring you the most comfort now and over the next few days. Rather than try to initiate new friendships, spend some quality time enjoying the people in your life. You might be up late if the drink flows and the conversation is gripping.

Thursday 27th

If there was a day to pull a sickie, this could be it. Certainly, you may find that being at home or with your family is emotionally comforting, whereas your stress levels could rise at work. The day is likely to get better as it goes on, as long as you put other people first.

Friday 28th

Try not to be overly stubborn around a family member.
You can dig in your heels and sometimes you may find it hard
to change your opinion. Now's the time to look again at a
family disagreement or home-related issue. It may not
matter who's right and who's wrong.

Saturday 29th

Start the bank holiday weekend by putting your feet up and
taking it easy. Being at home could be truly lovely as it allows
you to tap into your indulgent nature. This evening, a social
occasion piques your interest. If there's a whiff of romance in
the air, it's doubly appealing.

Sunday 30th

If you're a parent or have grandchildren, spend time with them
today. There's an easy flow and you'll enjoy being around their
fun and mischievous ways. Your Taurus nature loves to laugh
and you tend to have a great sense of humour. Indulge it to the
max and enjoy yourself.

MAY

. . . .

Monday 1st

You might be more than ready for an extra-long weekend. Taking time out could trigger a brainwave and help you realise how to deal with a challenging problem or work issue. Stay up late tonight as inspiration could strike close to when the clock strikes midnight.

Tuesday 2nd

Whatever you've decided about work or career, stick to your decision for now. However, you may want to keep your thoughts and feelings to yourself. There could be more that transpires over the next couple of weeks. Be resolute in your actions but don't reveal everything.

Wednesday 3rd

Keep life on an even keel at the moment. Someone close might be pushing you to tell them more about your situation, so try not to give in to their demands. When it comes to your work and your health, stick to your own counsel rather than ask for advice or suggestions.

Thursday 4th

You may have to learn to be more flexible and adaptable around money and the things that you value highly in life. Try to be philosophical about any changes taking place. Nothing is settled or stable now, so cheer your wins and come to terms with any losses.

Friday 5th

Take some time this weekend to ask yourself the key questions that are relevant in your life right now. For some of you, this will be about a close relationship, whether personal or professional. Big astrology is taking place that could indicate a significant turning point in your life.

Saturday 6th

Someone new could step into your life this weekend and turn things upside-down. This could be related to love but it might also be a teacher, a guru, or an inspirational friend. Other people are currently playing a powerful role in your life, sometimes too much so.

Sunday 7th

Your planet Venus is on the move today into caring, kind Cancer. It's a reminder to be around people you love and who love you in return. A conversation with a sibling or a neighbour who's become your confidante could help you make sense of recent events.

Monday 8th

You may be in a transitional phase now when you need to take a closer look at your financial and emotional ties. There's no need to rush into any major decisions but at least ensure that you're aware of any additional implications in these key areas.

Tuesday 9th

Trust your intuition in knowing what to do next. Decide about technology, what's working for you and what's not. You may be ready to do something radical or take a stand. You might choose to move away from social media or not attend a family event. It's your shout.

Wednesday 10th

You may need to re-establish your independence in one key area of your life. This may not go down well with everyone, perhaps a sibling or relative. Yet it's important to do what's right for you. Don't let another person's actions impact your life in a detrimental way.

Thursday 11th

You may be gearing up for a difficult conversation, but don't rush into things or allow yourself to come under pressure. Any big move on your part requires time and forethought so ensure you know what you're doing and why. Concentrate on your work as it can be a welcome escape.

Friday 12th

Consider your next steps carefully and notice where in life you feel out of sorts or unsettled. If your career or vocation doesn't match your bigger purpose, it could be glaringly obvious where change is required. Give yourself the weekend to think things through.

Saturday 13th

It's important to spend time with a family member who knows you best today. This might be a cousin who you used to hang out with years ago, or someone you see often. Whoever it is, lean on the person who supports you wholeheartedly.

Sunday 14th

You may be on the verge of making an important announcement or decision. If this is true for you, what you may need the most is a day with your best friends. Be with the people who've been by your side through thick and thin as they know you as no one else does.

Monday 15th

Today is a good time to sort out a misunderstanding that's taken place. Communication planet Mercury is direct, so voice your opinions and be clear about where you stand. It's time to find your voice, know what you want and why.

Tuesday 16th

Jupiter's change of star sign today is brimming with opportunity and good fortune for you. This is because, for the first time in twelve years, Jupiter enters Taurus. This is a positive time to put yourself first, line up a new plan for 2023 and beyond and keep your gaze firmly on the future.

Wednesday 17th

You may feel overwhelmed first thing but once the moon enters Taurus midday, your star is in the ascendancy. Whatever begins in your life now is worth taking note of because it promises success. Trust your luck and listen out for life's synchronicities stepping in to guide you.

Thursday 18th

It may be clear to you that it's time to close the door on one path in your life and embark on a new adventure. Consider where you're being called to step up or take on a leadership role. Where are you required to be powerful and where do you give your power away?

Friday 19th

Today's new moon in Taurus is brilliant for setting your intentions and looking at the year ahead. It would be a great weekend for mind-mapping and visualising what comes next. This is the time of the month to manifest your desires, so write them down or speak them out loud.

Saturday 20th

Action planet Mars enters your home and family zone and it's here where you're wise to channel your drive and ambition. Whether you're planning a move or you want to organise a family get-together, be proactive and make things happen. Do what you know is right.

Sunday 21st

It's never easy moving into a new phase in life. Yet, that may be what's required of you now. If you're not happy with your current path, stop and take some time out. You may move closer towards family and further away from a career goal.

Monday 22nd

Money could make all the difference to your next steps, your future plans. If you recognise that money brings you freedom, it might be time to step up and follow a new path. If you want to be there for someone in your family who's struggling financially, this too is an option.

Tuesday 23rd

Your generous gene is being triggered today. It may be hard for you to sit back and do nothing if you know that your contribution could make a huge difference to someone else's life. You're likely to step in and help but ensure you're doing it for the right reasons.

Wednesday 24th

You may be caught up in a family feud or find that doing the right thing for one person is the wrong thing as far as someone else is concerned. It's important to recognise that you're not going to be able to please everybody now. It's your decision that matters.

Thursday 25th

Have one final conversation and agree to disagree. The time is right to set new home and family initiatives in motion, especially if you know it will benefit more of you in the long run. For most of today, you have a free run to look after yourself and the ones you love.

Friday 26th

This is a good time to delve into the past. You could find that past connections crop up in unexpected ways. This might be the trigger for moving on and finding a way to be independent. A spontaneous act could work out for you romantically.

Saturday 27th

If there have been too many dramas in your life of late, perhaps involving your family or regarding where you live, you may be more than ready for a steady or stabilising influence to kick in. When in doubt, ensure you prioritise your children's needs above anyone else.

Sunday 28th

Try and make some final decisions this weekend. Focus on who or what's most important in your life and start from there. Even if you find yourself up against disapproval, it's the right time to make a strategic money move. Put your sound business head to good use.

Monday 29th

You may sense that you're out on your own at the moment but that's okay. When you focus on what you want rather than worrying too much about what other people think or need, it simplifies your progress. Do what's necessary to regain a sense of balance in your life.

Tuesday 30th

Aim to make logical and rational decisions now and you won't go far wrong. Leave emotions out of the equation and do what you know is right for you both financially and at work. If this benefits your family or improves your home situation, so much the better.

Wednesday 31st

Your nurturing nature is renowned, but you have a tough side too and can make firm decisions when necessary. Right now, it's important to maintain a sense of equilibrium and to keep things steady, both at work and concerning your health. Aim for stability in all areas.

JUNE

. . . .

Thursday 1st
You may choose to agree to disagree today. At work, it's important to realise that you don't always have to be on the same page. If you're meeting a loved one for lunch, the same applies. You could disagree over a home or family issue but don't let it spoil the mood.

Friday 2nd
You might be playing devil's advocate today in a close relationship. Ensure you check your motivations for doing so. What you see as a funny or a cheeky response might not be the same for everyone. This evening, you're able to smooth over any misunderstandings with ease.

Saturday 3rd
It's building up to be an intense weekend. It's not only a full moon weekend, which automatically heightens emotions but the moon is also in one of the most secretive and sensitive zones of your horoscope. This means life could be passionate but potentially argumentative too.

Sunday 4th
As an earth sign, security is important to you, both financial and emotional. Therefore, if you're currently undergoing a period of change regarding your money or your home, you may experience some feelings of worry or instability during this full moon phase. Keep your feet on the ground.

Monday 5th

Make home and family your priority from today onwards as
your planet Venus lights up this zone of your horoscope.
A tough decision could be on the cards, especially if events
at home impact your career and future path or vice versa.
You may be missing someone a lot.

Tuesday 6th

If you're full of clever ideas and witty repartee today, you're in
tune with your stars. Your ability to think on your feet and act
fast could be new, but can bring a sense of spontaneity and fun
to your day. You may stand up for your beliefs or principles.

Wednesday 7th

Watch out for issues of power or control that are getting out
of hand at work. You might be considering a radical move,
whether that means working from home or resigning from
your job. Over the next few months, your priority will more
likely be family than work.

Thursday 8th

It's not the easiest of days, especially if you're at odds with
other people, and this could be personal or professional. Most
likely, the issue is what you're doing for a job or the hours
you're working. Sometimes, you have to reach crisis point
before you're able to take action.

Friday 9th

Turn to your friends today for fun and advice. If it's been a
tricky week and you're finding it hard to know what to do
about a work or personal situation, hand it over to the people
who know you best. This evening is ideal for drinks and
laughter with your favourite friends.

Saturday 10th

Turn your attention towards your hopes and wishes and spend some time this weekend contemplating your future path. When your wants and needs are at odds with each other, you know that something needs to change. Be honest with yourself and do what's right.

Sunday 11th

It can be hard to let go of a goal or burning desire but it's important to consider whether you're on the right track. You may find the tough decision is taken out of your hands. Know that it's only when one door closes that a new door can open.

Monday 12th

Make the right move today, the one that benefits you financially. This could coincide with redundancy or a pay-out. You may have some concerns about what you're doing but, if in doubt, consider the beneficial impact that your decision will have on your family.

Tuesday 13th

There's no rush today, so pace yourself. You might be feeling vulnerable and would like some reassurance. If this is true, turn to the people you love. It's a good day to learn how to take care of yourself so put your needs first. You'll be back in the driving seat this evening.

Wednesday 14th

Know that you have a protective influence in your life now. The more you can trust and have faith that life will guide you, the smoother your progress. If a lot is going on at home or within your family, keep coming back to yourself and don't get pulled into any dramas.

Thursday 15th

Ring the changes and do something different. Sometimes, being spontaneous and shifting around your routine can have a beneficial effect on your well being. Money requires a sensible outlook but that's something you can do. Use your sound business head to make a wise decision.

Friday 16th

Be curious today and keep searching for new possibilities. This is especially important when it comes to money. You could profit from being a jack-of-all-trades and wheeling and dealing at a market or on the internet. Keep plotting and you'll soon be hurdling a current obstacle.

Saturday 17th

Get together with loved ones to have fun and help each other. The main topic of conversation may be money if someone's doing well or a relationship is prospering. There could be issues with an old friend in your life. Be there for them.

Sunday 18th

Today's new moon is a symbol of new beginnings and it falls in your money zone. This is a great date to set your intentions around money, write an abundance cheque and voice your wishes to the universe. It's a good date to take the initiative and set new plans in motion.

Monday 19th

If you're looking for an escape from the everyday, turn to your friends for guidance and wisdom. Find your escape without losing yourself. A recurring disappointment could crop up. Make key connections that could help resolve a current issue or ease unsettled feelings.

Tuesday 20th

The moon in Cancer is a kind and caring influence. Therefore, notice where you can make a difference today. A kind word, a nod or smile may mean more to someone than you may know. Trust your intuition in reaching out to others and let go of a personal disappointment.

Wednesday 21st

Today is the solstice, and the Sun's move into Cancer lights up your communication zone. This includes the written and spoken word. Whether you're interacting more with your siblings or neighbours, it's a good time to reach out to others and join in with your local community.

Thursday 22nd

You may be planning a family get-together, whether a wedding or big anniversary is coming up. If so, this could keep you busy over the next few weeks. There's passion and intensity at home or with your loved ones. Enjoy what's going on but make time for yourself as well.

Friday 23rd

As you head into the weekend, line up some social events with your favourite people. Aim for a slower pace and go with the flow. Being with children could help to ground you and you might be keen to meet up with your siblings or relatives. Aim for less drama, more calm.

Saturday 24th

The moon is in an earth sign for most of the weekend.
This would be a good time to head out into the countryside
or to be in nature. If you have a garden, spend time with your
feet on the earth and aim to sit and do nothing for an hour or
two. Relax and enjoy yourself.

Sunday 25th

You may be worried about a friend today, especially if they're
having a tough time financially. Let your emotions flow if
necessary and try to come up with an easy solution to their
dilemma. Get your thinking hat on when you're pondering in
the garden or chilling out.

Monday 26th

It takes a lot for you to get angry but you may feel frustrated
today and tempers could flare. Try not to get overly involved
with someone close and take a step back from a challenging
family situation. Avoid any road rage when you're out and
about and walk away instead.

Tuesday 27th

Mercury's move into Cancer today turns your attention
towards your siblings, neighbours and the local community.
Keep the lines of communication open and make an extra
effort to connect with people in your vicinity and create a
strong neighbourhood network. You're stronger together.

Wednesday 28th

Put some time and effort into close relationships today and you'll be rewarded. It's important to be honest about your feelings and not veer away from strong emotions. If you're looking for love, it's a good day to reach out to someone close or line up a first date.

Thursday 29th

It's a positive day to deal with administration or paperwork and get on top of information. Put your mind to it and you could tick quite a few items off your to-do list. If you have to make a choice this evening between love or friendship, opt for the person you've known the longest.

Friday 30th

A conversation or situation with a good friend could take up a lot of your time now. It's important, however, especially if your friend is dealing with an emotional crisis or you're concerned they're not telling the truth. Don't hold on to a fixed outcome and go with the flow.

JULY

. . . .

Saturday 1st

If you're awake early this morning, take advantage of the
sunrise and get out for an early walk. A magical message could
be delivered to you when you pay close attention around 5 am.
All day is looking good for receiving good news, compliments
or gifts. Bask in good vibes.

Sunday 2nd

It's not like you to crave independence but your stars currently
favour freedom. You may be sensing the full-moon vibe that's
growing and heightening emotions, and this might help you
to realise that you need to distance yourself from a family
situation that's turning out to be overly dramatic.

Monday 3rd

Today's full moon lights up your travel and study zone and
you might be determined to try again with a life-long dream.
This could be emigration, a sabbatical from work or
committing to a course of study. Even if your options are
limited, that doesn't mean you should stop exploring.

Tuesday 4th

You might be tempted to pursue a spiritual path or be open to
a new religion. Ask yourself why certain areas of your life are
opening up for you now. Which dreams are possible and which
do you need to say goodbye to? Or, at least put on the back
burner for now.

Wednesday 5th

It could be challenging to listen to your head first, your heart second. Yet this is what's required if you're going to be able to get on with work or hold down a job. Be logical and rational about what you're doing and create new systems to help you stay on track.

Thursday 6th

Your relationships at home or within your family are fizzing with energy. This could mean that a lot is happening or you may be caught up in the middle of a drama. Park your emotions for now, especially if you have a lot to do on the computer or regarding your work.

Friday 7th

Events first thing could determine the course of your day. You might answer a call for help, or you could be the one who reaches out spontaneously and decides to prioritise socialising over work and chores. Technology can speed up your progress. Meet up with friends later on.

Saturday 8th

An early-morning run or a breakfast date would be a great way to start the day. Leap into action and do something fun and alternative. Be with a friend who inspires you or someone who knows how to help you access your emotions. A night on your own could be restorative.

Sunday 9th

If you've got a busy week coming up or you're getting ready for a holiday, do yourself a favour and free up your schedule. Find time to recharge your batteries and get organised. If you want to catch up with a close friend or relative, find time to speak later this evening.

Monday 10th

Make a commitment to yourself that you'll prioritise all the good things in your life from today onwards. This includes creative projects and hobbies, entertainment, romance and spending time with your children. A talk or social event could be cancelled this evening so be flexible.

Tuesday 11th

Communication planet Mercury whizzes into your home and family zone for a quick two-week stay. This is great for opening the lines of communication and keeping your family relationships light. There may be a lot to talk or gossip about due to recent events. Engage with your loved ones.

Wednesday 12th

It's potentially a good day for getting on top of technology or updating your phone or means of communication. Yet there's restless energy and you need an outlet for your hyperactive mind. If you have a yearning to be a rebel or activist, here's your opportunity.

Thursday 13th

You may have to come up with some innovative ideas on how to pay for a hobby, social event or a special occasion. Juggle different options and see which one fits the best. If you're a parent, talk to relatives about a child's fundraising efforts or helping out with their education.

Friday 14th

You may be aware of the kindness of strangers today. Whether someone steps in to help or you have a fascinating conversation, be on the lookout for the unexpected. Rather than keep your head down and mind your own business, be more engaged with the people around you.

Saturday 15th

There are some days when it's important to know that you're valued and the people you love appreciate you. Rather than stay silent, ask for an opinion or a compliment. It's a good day to spend money on your home or family, just as long as you pool resources.

Sunday 16th

The more people you see today, the better. It's a fine day for communication, connections and networking. Get out and about in your local community, attend your church or join in with a neighbourhood event. You may discover you can be helpful in more ways than one.

Monday 17th

Today's new moon falls in your communication zone, which means the coming week is great for updating technology, buying a phone or sorting out your mode of transport. This is even more important if a key piece of equipment needs replacing. If it's broken, get it fixed.

Tuesday 18th

You may have a lot going on this summer. Perhaps you're renovating or you have people coming to stay. You might be catching up with family you haven't seen for a while or arranging a big event. Move fast and get things organised.

Wednesday 19th

You might be on the phone with tradesmen or builders today, or catching up with a sibling or relative. Any forms of communication that help you make swift progress at home or within your family are well-starred. Crack on with these key areas of your life.

Thursday 20th

You may feel disappointed with someone today, perhaps a child or lover. Or, you're required to step in and be there for someone you love who's currently struggling. Keep firm boundaries in place, but, at the same time, offer as much kindness and caring as you're able.

Friday 21st

Family connections are important now and it could be an emotional or sentimental time. Yet you're advised not to let other people hold you back, however much you care for them. This could be a tricky line to hold, but navigate your close relationships as smoothly as you can.

Saturday 22nd

This would be a good date to make a key decision about travel or study plans. This may mean that you postpone or cancel a trip or course. Accept what's not working out, however challenging this may be. A clean sweep could encourage fresh energy and new ideas to come in.

Sunday 23rd

Home and family affairs are under the cosmic spotlight. If you're moving home, you might feel sad that you're leaving your neighbours or relatives behind. Alternatively, you may be upset with someone close and decide that it would be best to take a temporary break from one another.

Monday 24th

If the weekend's events turned out to be dramatic, focus on calming things down today. Aim for balance and harmony in your life, whatever that takes. Eat well, be healthy and prioritise exercise. Get organised at work and fit in with the team. Let any turbulent emotions settle.

Tuesday 25th

You may receive some good advice today from a colleague or someone you know through sport or exercise. It could be helpful to hear an objective opinion about a personal or family issue. That doesn't mean you'll like what you hear, but at least be willing to listen.

. . . .

Wednesday 26th

Encourage a child or lover to open up today and express their emotions. If someone's taken the brave step of seeing a counsellor or therapist, be supportive of their choice. If you're on a date this evening, find out more about the other person and reveal less about yourself.

Thursday 27th

It's the perfect date to catch up and talk with family. If there's been a recent issue or falling-out, know that it might take a while for the situation to be resolved. It's a similar scenario if you're in the process of buying or selling property. Any hold-ups could delay a project until September.

Friday 28th

It's important to do more of what you love and less of what you don't this weekend. Focus on your areas of expertise, your skills and talents and how you express yourself. When you make happiness a priority, things fall into place more easily. Consider what this means for you.

Saturday 29th

It's a gorgeous date for love and romance or re-establishing the bonds of connection between you and a family member. Emotions could feel intense but give in to your feelings and don't repress them. Let someone know how much you care about them and be open to love.

Sunday 30th

As one of the earth signs, it's important that you make time for activities that ground you. The quickest and easiest way to do this is to go for a walk in nature. Be around comfort and familiarity, and enjoy yourself with family or friends who know you well.

Monday 31st

It's a lovely start to the week. You're wise to ensure that the people you love the most are doing well, especially if someone close needs reassurance. This might concern a child or lover in your life. Be a solid role model for others, an anchor that holds everyone steady.

AUGUST

Tuesday 1st

If things aren't harmonious at home, today's full moon could represent a turning point or watershed. Full moons bring things to light and heighten emotions. This could be a powerful full moon for your career or vocation when you're ready to make a big decision.

Wednesday 2nd

Steer clear of negativity today and distance yourself from anyone in your life who puts you down or dismisses your ideas. If you know what's right for you to find happiness, that's what matters most. Make up your mind when it comes to matters of the heart.

Thursday 3rd

You may have to step in to help out a child today, perhaps because they're having friendship issues. Ideally, advise them on how to deal with the situation and ensure you remind them of their self-worth in the process. In affairs of the heart, keep love and friendship separate.

Friday 4th

It may hurt to receive a rejection but at least you know where you stand. Saying nothing won't get you anywhere and you may find out more in the process. If you're going out tonight, it's likely to be a late one. The cinema or a wine bar would be the ideal location.

Saturday 5th

You may want to chill out today. You do have a lazy side to your nature and it could do you the world of good to put your feet up and take it easy. Think of this as a chance to recharge your batteries. Build some much-needed me time into your schedule.

Sunday 6th

Look after yourself today and indulge in self-care. If there's someone you're looking after, perhaps a parent or elderly person, it could be a lovely day to hang out with them. Avoid any stress and do whatever makes you feel good. If you have an eye for design, rearrange your surroundings.

Monday 7th

If you haven't been paying enough attention to yourself recently, now's the time to readdress the balance. You might be keen to make steady progress with a personal goal or target. You may recognise that it might be the right time to give your image or profile a boost.

Tuesday 8th

Your stars indicate that it's a good day for entrepreneurial activities. Whatever goal you've been visualising recently, be bold and take a risk. The stronger your self-belief, the easier it will be to fulfil your true potential. Embrace an adventure and make an independent move.

Wednesday 9th

It's important to recognise when your intervention can make a difference and when it's best to leave well alone. This is about your home and family situation. Be clear about your motivations for stepping in if someone's behaving erratically. Single? It might be worth staying up late for love.

Thursday 10th

Focus on enjoyment and what makes you happy and make a commitment to yourself to do more. You might be prepared to spend more money than usual to pursue a good time. Whether your priority is romance, children, entertainment or a creative project, leap to it.

Friday 11th

You'll make things easier now if you consider your spending habits carefully. If you're in a relationship or you live with your family, it's a good day for investing in these areas or doing something special together. What won't go down well is spending money solely on yourself.

Saturday 12th

Deepen your connections today and get to know someone better. This might be a neighbour or someone you meet in your local community. You may be asked to step into a teaching role or to take on a position of leadership, perhaps as a governor in your local school.

Sunday 13th

It's a lovely day for a reunion and making connections. You could hear from a childhood sweetheart or catch up with someone you knew when you were young. Alternatively, spend a quiet day at home with the one you love and remind yourself of what attracts you to each other.

Monday 14th

Your major astrology this week is taking place in Leo, the star sign at the base of your horoscope. Leo rules your home and family, your past and where you come from. It's where you discover your roots and your security. Turn your attention to these key areas of life.

Tuesday 15th

You may feel tremendous pride today for a child or a member of your family. If you're in a loving relationship, your emotions could be expansive as if your heart might burst with pleasure. Let someone know how much you care about them and be open with your feelings.

Wednesday 16th

Today's new moon is ideal for delving into the past. You may find that past connections crop up. This could be a time when you're on the move and seeking ways to be more independent. Your current stars are encouraging you to do things your way.

Thursday 17th

You're in the mood to play today, which means it might not be easy if you're at work or dealing with responsibilities. If you love the job you do, be creative and playful in your work and your partnerships. If a child's feeling down, you may know exactly how to cheer them up.

Friday 18th

Focus on your areas of expertise, your skills and talents and how you express yourself. When you seek enjoyment in life and make happiness a priority, things tend to fall into place more easily. It doesn't matter whether you're at work or home, bring your best self to the table.

Saturday 19th

The joy of creativity is to be found in the activity rather than the result. It's important to remember this if you're disappointed with how a project turns out. Once you share your art or craft with others, you may realise that a lot depends on the person doing the observing.

Sunday 20th

Pay close attention to your health and well-being, especially if you've been overly indulgent of late. It's a good day to eat well, catch up on your sleep and take some exercise. Encourage your family to do the same and have fun in the process. Teamwork reaps rewards.

Monday 21st

It's an excellent day for getting organised whether at home or in the office. Catch up with paperwork and filing and ensure your surroundings are beautiful and harmonious. You might not be up for much this evening but make the most of a relaxing vibe in the daytime.

Tuesday 22nd

Your relationships may be on fire today but there could be too much emotion for you or someone close to handle. Enjoy being with the one you love rather than questioning whether you're reading from the same page. It's a time to feel deeply rather than dissect what love means.

Wednesday 23rd

Prioritise earthy activities over the next few weeks and do more of what grounds you. This might include cooking and eating well, gardening and harvesting food, having or giving a massage or going out for regular walks in the country.

Thursday 24th

Mercury is now retrograde and one of the best ways to use this phase is to work less, play more. This could be a reflective and thoughtful time when you're pondering what happiness means. For you, it could be a love affair, a creative project or your relationship with a child.

Friday 25th

Be around the ones you love, especially your children or a lover and people whose company you enjoy. All the earth signs favour laughter and humour and the focus remains on play rather than work. Alternatively, make your working life a place of joy if you're busy.

Saturday 26th

You may be feeling doubtful first thing or be guilty about a love relationship. Your emotions could be out of sorts so it's best not to dive in deep. Later on, busy yourself with a project that helps to ground you. Get your friends involved and create a masterpiece together.

Sunday 27th

Lifestyle and routine can play a big part in your wellbeing. Consider how you spend your days and how you approach life on a daily level. What makes you feel good? Ask yourself what you can do to make your life easier and be more in flow?'

Monday 28th

Your stars are ideal for bank holiday Monday whether you're on holiday, coming back from a trip or enjoying a day relaxing and taking it easy. It will be harder than usual to turn your attention to work and serious issues. If you can get organised this evening, it's worth it.

Tuesday 29th

You might have to drag yourself back to work today. Ideally, you'll be taking advantage of a break from your routine and be able to ring the changes in a different location. If you're typical of your star sign, you can get stuck in a rut, but right now you may be craving something different.

Wednesday 30th

It may be hard not to act spontaneously now. You could expose your rebel tendencies and refuse to stick to the rules. Doing what you're told won't come easily. This could trigger a challenging situation at work. A good friend may try to talk some sense into you this evening.

Thursday 31st

Today's full moon is ideal for trusting your intuition and making a spontaneous or impulsive move, perhaps when it comes to your friends or your creative projects. There could be news of a pregnancy or a major announcement from a child. Love too is in the ascendancy.

SEPTEMBER

. . . .

Friday 1st

If you have the full moon blues first thing, consider changing things around so you do less not more today. You might be feeling weepy or emotional about a friend. Slow things down and put your needs first. This may mean putting off date night or spending time alone.

Saturday 2nd

You won't have to wait much longer to find out more about a home or family issue that's been delayed. There's a turning point on the way before too long. Be gentle with yourself and other people today. Take time out to rest and retreat and practise stillness.

Sunday 3rd

If things don't work out well today, this could be the trigger for an emotional release. Know that come the afternoon you'll start to perk up and your confidence will rise. If you're waiting to hear from someone and you're becoming impatient, you might be blessed with good news later on.

Monday 4th

The planet of love and connection, Venus, turns direct today. Therefore, this isn't the time to go it alone. Instead, reach out to others and find yourself through your connections. This could indicate a change of heart in home and family-related matters, as new beginnings open up.

Tuesday 5th

There may be an issue around following the rules or
questioning leadership today. You want to find your way
and do what's right for you. Be questioning and don't accept
everything you're told. Other people may turn to you for help.
Your advice and guidance could be in demand.

Wednesday 6th

Your close connections are powerful. This includes your
relationship with children as a parent, grandparent, godparent,
auntie, uncle or teacher. You can inspire and teach the young
now whether you do this for a living or not. Keep your money
in your pocket and offer advice instead.

Thursday 7th

You may be hoping for a stroke of luck or good fortune coming
your way. If money's a worry, it could be affecting your sleep.
The good news is that better times are on the way, but it starts
with gratitude and acceptance for what you have in your life.

Friday 8th

You have lucky stars today. This is the perfect time to prioritise
pleasure and do more of what you love. It's a good day for
risk-taking and worth a flutter. Look out for new opportunities
that come your way. You might be proud of a child or meet
someone irresistible.

Saturday 9th

You could gain kudos for an artistic or creative achievement
today or get tickets for a much-desired form of entertainment.
The more you put into life, the more you get back, so this isn't
the weekend to sit and do nothing. Instead, make the most of
some positive vibes.

Sunday 10th

You may be full of great ideas today and it's an ideal Sunday to meet up with other people and keep the lines of communication open. Talk to people who inspire you, check out an event in your local neighbourhood and meet people of like minds. Enjoy your life close to home.

Monday 11th

It's time to pick up where you left off concerning a home move or a family get-together. If there was a delay over the summer, get back on track with your goals and plans. If there was a misunderstanding, it's an ideal day to reach out and heal a family rift.

Tuesday 12th

You might have taken on a new role within your family, the awakener. You're no longer prepared to let things be and you're more motivated to engage directly with any issues or challenges. Not everyone will appreciate the new you, but do what feels right for the current situation.

Wednesday 13th

If you're worried about someone close who's feeling down or low, perhaps a child or lover, don't leave your thoughts unsaid. Pick up the phone or have a heart-to-heart this evening. Ask the right questions and you'll quickly discover what's underneath their mood.

Thursday 14th

It's always easier being around other people who are in a good mood. Positive vibes are attractive and catching and can't help but cheer you up. Whether you're the one who's playing cheerleader or you're the one attracting laughter and compliments, it's a lovely feel-good day.

Friday 15th

Your creativity is in full swing during today's new moon so tap into the artistic side of your nature. The more you put into your life outside of your work, the better. Unless your current job or vocation is your passion. If so, then happy days.

Saturday 16th

Mercury's change of direction is your cue to pick up the phone and reach out. You might discover more about a love affair and whether it's on or off. You could have a pleasing encounter with a child or someone dear to your heart. Be wary of an emotional outburst this evening.

Sunday 17th

Your indulgent nature is in full swing today and you might be feeling chuffed with yourself if a romantic relationship is going well. It's a good day to reach out to other people or spend quality time with your partner. The two of you could find more than one way to connect.

Monday 18th

Turn your attention to your one-to-ones, your close relationships. If you've not been spending much time with someone close, consider how you can readdress the balance. You could decide to make some long-term plans together. Passion is potentially on the cards this evening.

Tuesday 19th

Someone could lead you astray today if you don't have a strong sense of your identity. Be self-aware and realise that not everyone has your best interests at heart. Alternatively, if you're sure of yourself and a romantic relationship, you may be more than ready to give in to romance.

Wednesday 20th

A loving relationship could bring a lot of joy into your life now. This might be your marriage or a romantic relationship. Alternatively, you could be spending more time with another individual who means a lot to you. This evening, you may be loathe to deal with a serious issue.

Thursday 21st

You may need assistance today if you're trying to find a way to fund an experience for yourself, a child or a lover in your life. Reach out to your partner or relatives and widen your circle of opportunity. The more people involved, the easier it will be to reach a funding target.

Friday 22nd

You may be experiencing some financial concerns. You might be worried about savings or debt, especially if you don't have all the information to hand. Make a plan rather than get into a panic and make a real effort to find out more.

Saturday 23rd

The Sun's move into Libra today shifts the emphasis from play to work in your horoscope. This is where balance can be found, focusing on your daily routine, your lifestyle and your health. It's an ideal opportunity to get on track with new habits that can boost your wellbeing.

Sunday 24th

Take yourself off somewhere different and expand your horizons. If you're not looking forward to going back to work tomorrow, even more reason to ring the changes today. It's a good day to look into holiday plans for 2024. Browse some travel websites this evening.

Monday 25th

At work, this is an ideal time to widen your network, hone your people skills and make new connections. Teamwork and partnership can help you progress faster than going it alone. If you're looking for work, now's the time to send off an application or rewrite your CV.

Tuesday 26th

It might be harder than usual to concentrate at work today. You could be pulled back towards your home or family life, for whatever reason. Use the internet to speed up your progress and multi-task rather than try to stick to a single project. You might get more done.

Wednesday 27th

Ensure you keep firm boundaries in place when it comes to friendship or a group in which you're involved. It would be easy to give a lot but this could be tiring or exhausting in the long run. If you feel obliged to help out, your only option may be to knuckle down and get on with it.

Thursday 28th

Your concentration levels may be all over the place today. If so, know that this week's full moon could shed light on your situation and bring a turning point. Consider what you might need to let go of or where you've been burning the candle at both ends.

Friday 29th

Today's full moon highlights your work, lifestyle and service to others. You may be juggling the work/life balance or want to prioritise your health. Something could come to an end now that may benefit you in the long run. It might free up a situation in which you feel trapped.

Saturday 30th

It will be frustrating if you have to work today. Try and do so graciously rather than be in a bad mood. Ideally, you want some time to chill out and rest. Someone close will cheer you up later on. A child or lover could be the person who puts a smile on your face.

OCTOBER

· · · · · · · · · · · · · · · · · ·

Sunday 1st

The less you have scheduled today, the better. It's important to catch up with what you want to do if you were working yesterday. As one of the earth signs, you need time out more than most so try not to get caught up on the hamster wheel of life. Tap back into your dreams.

Monday 2nd

You may have the energy and confidence now to believe you can achieve anything. Use visualisation techniques to stay on track with your inner purpose and deepen your self-belief. Aim high in life and don't settle for second best. You know you deserve more.

Tuesday 3rd

Your great gift is making things happen and this is an excellent day to tackle a money issue. A late start could throw you but you'll get back on track. This evening, make time for a child or lover, especially if they're on the verge of making a final decision about their next steps.

Wednesday 4th

Set your priorities at work today and be productive as you tick things off your to-do list. Make sure you have the financial resources lined up for what you want to do next. Use your people skills to charm others into your way of thinking and big yourself up.

Thursday 5th

Communication planet Mercury enters Libra and your work and health zone's today. This gives you the gift of the gab and it's a good day to arrange a meeting, interview or medical appointment. Another person's advice could prove invaluable, so reach out and ask for an expert opinion.

Friday 6th

If you've arranged a lunchtime rendezvous, be aware that you might not have enough time to make it happen. Work could get exceptionally busy, and your help might be required by another person in your team. Don't worry overly, as you'll get a chance to catch up later on.

Saturday 7th

You could be running here, there and everywhere today with errands or chauffeuring duties. If you're catching up with a sibling, relative or neighbour, do so earlier rather than later. Leave it until the evening and arguments are more likely.

Sunday 8th

You might enjoy catching up with family today or be feeling proud if you're in a brand new home. It wasn't the easiest summer for home and family affairs but you're likely to feel pleased if you're settling into a new phase. You could be helping someone close find a job.

Monday 9th

Venus's move today is helpful after recent dramas. Turn your attention to the small things, everything that gives you joy. Bring it back to what you can see, hear, feel or touch. Enjoy a sunset, play with a child or be open to love.

Tuesday 10th

Don't rush into a new relationship but take your time. This is especially important if you're aware that you're leaping in too soon. If you're a parent, a child may need extra guidance today. Don't be scared of laying down new rules or guidelines if you believe it's necessary.

Wednesday 11th

You could have a big decision to make about travel or study this week. One project or plan may be put on hold when life intervenes. Be patient if this is the case and don't force the issue. Aim to try again next year if you're not accepted on an educational course.

Thursday 12th

Action planet Mars enters your relationship zone. Cue more passion but potentially more arguments too. Other people are strong, which is good news if you're in a relationship and want your partner to step up. This could be the start of a new love adventure.

Friday 13th

A partnership is the key to your success. It's about making the right connections and getting the best advice. You could quickly realise who's the best person for the job, whether you're looking for someone to help you out personally or professionally. Check out their references.

Saturday 14th

Eclipses bring what's hidden to light and today's powerful solar eclipse represents an ending and a beginning. This is to do with your lifestyle so it could be about giving up a habit, doing less of what's bad for you and more of what's good for you.

Sunday 15th

This eclipse weekend could herald a sea-change for the job or role you do every day. Notice the conversations you have around work and health. What gets seeded could stir your dreams and get you fired up for new beginnings. Your passionate nature is in overdrive this evening.

Monday 16th

It would be easy to let someone else take the lead today, at work or at home. Before this happens, be clear about their motivations and dig a little deeper. If you're giving away your freedom in the process, it might be best to share things.

Tuesday 17th

You could get to know someone in your life on a deeper level today. Explore some topics of interest that you've never touched on before and find out about their beliefs or political views. This evening, don't be hard on yourself if you're disheartened about a financial issue.

Wednesday 18th

It would be easy to compare yourself detrimentally to others today but this isn't wise. It doesn't help anyone, least of all you. When it comes to your relationship with a child or lover, be clear with them about what you can and can't afford. Honesty is your best policy.

Thursday 19th

If you're feeling disillusioned about the promise of a pay rise or another source of income that hasn't materialised, get talking. When you open up about a financial matter, you may discover there's a chance to take on some overtime or apply for a new job or position.

. . . .

Friday 20th

Get serious about your work goals and line up an important meeting or interview. Ask for what you want and you'll soon be standing on firmer ground. This evening is gorgeous for a date with a difference. Do something you haven't done before with the one you love.

Saturday 21st

This could turn out to be a big weekend. You might realise that staying in the same job forever won't fulfil your dreams. Perhaps you recognise that it's time to take better care of your body and your health. A crisis or wake-up call could be the catalyst that springs you into action.

Sunday 22nd

You may encounter a new business partner today or find the person you've been looking for to help you with a personal goal. This could be a time of deep healing and transformation when it comes to love. If a new romance begins, it's the right relationship for you.

Monday 23rd

The Sun's move into Scorpio today highlights your relationships. If you've been waiting for some time to find love or for love to find you, here's your opportunity. Create deep connections with other people as this is soulmate territory. Get the right professional experts on your team.

Tuesday 24th

You may be experiencing some super passionate vibes this week as Scorpio season kicks in. Superficial gossip is out, deep and meaningful conversations are in. Meet up with a good friend today and the two of you can put the world to rights. Talk about real issues.

Wednesday 25th

Your friends are a gold mine of advice and ideas. This is especially true if you're looking for guidance regarding a romantic relationship or a situation with a child. You'll have a great time today if you're celebrating a friend's birthday or toasting their success.

Thursday 26th

Pay close attention to your dreams and write down any insights first thing as this could prove revealing. There's a theme of secrets and confidences in your astrology and you may not be ready to tell all. You might still be coming to terms with what's going on in your private life.

Friday 27th

If you can create some time to be by yourself today, do so. This is especially important if you've recently dived into a passionate liaison that's taken over your life. Alternatively, you might be worn out if you've been around a lot of people recently. Some quiet time may be required.

Saturday 28th

Today's lunar eclipse takes place in your star sign. Therefore, you immediately know that this is going to be an important weekend for you. Whatever your current relationship situation, an eclipse promises drama and excitement, or important lessons around partnership.

Sunday 29th

You may be up against opposition today, or you're comparing yourself to other peoples' achievements. Either way, take a step back and use your common sense to decide what's next rather than leap into a lively partnership situation all guns blazing.

Monday 30th

Now's the time to reassess your one-to-ones as new information comes to light. Decide where your heart lies and firm up your boundaries around love and partnership. Be with people who buoy you up rather than bring you down. Avoid power games in the office.

Tuesday 31st

If you're caught in a triangle situation, it may be time to decide who's right for you. A love affair could be catapulted into the public arena and you have to declare your true affections. If you're single, get yourself to a Halloween party as love is calling.

NOVEMBER

Wednesday 1st

If you sound like a broken record when it comes to a money issue and keep repeating the same thing, try something different today. Look at your situation from a fresh perspective rather than believe everything you hear or read. It's a lovely evening to catch up with an old friend.

Thursday 2nd

Make time for an easy conversation today and catch up with people who live close by. Talk to people you meet whether you're out on a dog walk or doing your local shopping. Community matters, and you may hear about a new neighbourhood initiative that you would like to join.

Friday 3rd

Your relationships could feel like a struggle today. Perhaps you and someone close are not on the same wavelength. Rather than beat your head against a brick wall, take a step back and follow your agenda. The last thing you want is to come across as desperate or disinterested.

Saturday 4th

If a responsible role is more of a burden than a joy, you may consider stepping down and handing over the reins to someone else. Relationships remain edgy and it's not the best time to try to sort things out. Say less rather than more and go about your daily business instead.

Sunday 5th

Avoid a family get-together today and don't feel obliged to spend time with your in-laws. Close relationships remain testing and it might be wise to point out who's being stubborn about an ongoing issue. Sometimes, a clash can clear the air or it digs you deeper into a hole.

Monday 6th

Try not to let a drama or issue that cropped up over the weekend stray into your working week. Close the door on any problem areas and focus on what is going well in your life. If you're proud of a child, let them know. They may be moving schools or starting a new job.

Tuesday 7th

If romance is lacking from a relationship, speak words of love and see what happens. Sometimes, all it takes is a loving text or saying I'm sorry to heal a rift or personal issue. Actively pursue the things in life that please you. This might be a hobby or spending quality time with a child.

Wednesday 8th

Your planet Venus enters Libra today. This reorients your focus towards your work and your health. Seek balance and harmony in these key areas. Work could be a welcome escape from a challenging personal life. Look after your body, pay attention to your mind and boost your spirits.

Thursday 9th

Being around people who are easy to get on with could act as a soothing balm. Veer towards the team who work well together, complementing each other's skills. This may be at work or a sport that you love. Aim for peace and harmony in your life.

Friday 10th

You could argue over money today, perhaps with a friend or loved one. If you're spending too much on a group or club, or you want to help out another friend financially, this could be the trigger. Slow things down if necessary and work out your next steps thoughtfully.

Saturday 11th

You are one of the most patient of all the star signs. However, even you may feel the heat if you are inundated with requests and demands from other people. One relationship might be unusually feisty. This could be your cue to break away from a relationship that's out of balance.

Sunday 12th

Don't expect other people to be reliable now or even behave well. Tempers may flare. If your buttons are pressed, you could act impulsively. Yet look out for the unexpected too. Someone new entering your life could turn things around or even upside-down in a good way.

Monday 13th

What takes place on or around today's new moon in your relationship zone promises to be exciting for love one way or another. Check out someone new who enters your life or re-engage with a relationship that has lost it's way. It's a good new moon for starting over.

Tuesday 14th

There may be a specific reason why you're dealing with a lot of people. Perhaps, you're expanding your business or you've recently taken on a new role. Be tolerant but assertive. Your planet Venus was not only sweet and kind but a warrior too.

. . . .

Wednesday 15th

It's an excellent day for a meeting or interview related to work or money. Talk to a bank manager if you're considering a loan or mortgage. You may be hiring and firing. Or, maybe there's someone who's piqued your interest at work for other reasons.

Thursday 16th

After recent drama or excitement, it's time to feel the earth beneath your feet and slow down the pace. Spend time today with the people who know you best, your oldest friends or someone you knew when you were a student. Look to the future and line up some new plans.

Friday 17th

If you want more romance in your life, sometimes the easiest way to achieve this is to start by being more romantic yourself. Buy flowers or chocolates today for that someone special. If you're looking for love, be flirtatious and let someone know you care. Give in to romance.

Saturday 18th

Now is not the time for words but the time for action. Decide what this means for you concerning a close relationship. Passion is a strong possibility and intimacy could immediately be connecting. If you're caught up in a competitive situation, don't go overboard today.

Sunday 19th

You might be busy on the computer today, whether you've recently joined a dating app or you're catching up with work or correspondence. Turn your attention towards your goals and spend some time deciding whether you're on the right path regarding your career or vocation.

Monday 20th

You may run into someone at work who loves power.
Rather than overreact, take a step back and distance yourself.
Stay focused on what you need to do and let them know calmly
that you don't require their input. Carefully consider whether
the boss needs to be aware.

Tuesday 21st

A group event could be stimulating today and give you lots
of inspiration. Whether you're at a workshop or in a team
meeting, engage with other people and share your ideas.
This evening, try not to get involved in an ongoing discussion
about money with a friend.

Wednesday 22nd

The Sun moves into your money zone, highlighting joint
finances and shared resources. Crack on with money matters,
whether you're dealing with an inheritance, mortgage, loan,
savings, debt or taxes. Play your cards right and you could
transform a financial situation over the next month.

Thursday 23rd

You may run into an obstacle today and this is linked to what
you're trying to do financially. Don't let this stop you, but do
be aware you might need to pace yourself and reassess what's
possible in the time you have available. Slow and steady wins
the race.

Friday 24th

Resolve to put any arguments or tensions behind you. This is your cosmic cue to let go of jealousy or obsessive behaviour. Create relationships in your life that are based on freedom and trust. Your money motivation will be revved up once again from today.

Saturday 25th

This is a great time for money initiatives and attacking your financial situation head-on. Think about your security and consider what you need to do to improve your current situation. You may have to make a tough decision to secure the future you want for yourself and your family.

Sunday 26th

You're at your best when you have a safe harbour, a place where you feel comfortable and at home. What you may realise now is that this has less to do with money than you perhaps imagined. It's an ideal time to reassess your values and where you find self-worth.

Monday 27th

This could turn out to be a big week concerning money and finances. Today's full moon highlights the financial axis of your horoscope so trust your intuition in knowing what to do. Balance your head and your heart when making a clear and bold cash decision. Trust yourself.

Tuesday 28th

Try not to be overly romantic around money. Ensure you keep your earthy common sense intact and don't get carried away on a whim or a hope. Someone could promise a lot but deliver little. Be wary of helping someone out financially if the boundaries aren't clearly defined.

Wednesday 29th

Engage your curiosity and get your brain working. You may join forces with a good friend or someone in your local community. You might be teaching or passing on your wisdom or expertise. You may not need to read more as you already have the knowledge you require.

Thursday 30th

It's a lively day for communication and making connections. Step out of your comfort zone and approach someone whose style you like. This could benefit you personally or professionally. Engage in a new activity that keeps your mind lively, like a puzzle book.

DECEMBER

· · · · · · · · · · · · · · · · · · ·

Friday 1st

You may have a lot to talk about or think about from today onwards and new ideas could be buzzing around. Your focus is on the future, whether you're considering next year's holiday or finding out more about an educational course. Relax at home this evening.

Saturday 2nd

If you're typical of your star sign, you'll love considering your long-term goals and how you're going to work towards them. Get a good friend involved whether you'd like a trip away or you're considering a festive break abroad. Ensure that your family are on board with your plans.

Sunday 3rd

Your planet Venus remains in the sign of balanced Libra until tomorrow. The theme is moderation and not getting carried away. This applies to your work and routine, your lifestyle and your health. Don't take work home with you today and try not to fall into unhealthy habits.

Monday 4th

Today's stars are powerful and there may be a chance to transform a relationship for the better. You might be enamoured with a teacher or coach, or fall in love with someone exciting, passionate or profound. Dive deeply into life and find where magic and mystery lie.

Tuesday 5th

When it comes to your romantic relationships, today's theme is commitment and discussing future plans. If you're in a new relationship, let them know your true feelings. If you're single, get together with a good friend and join a dating app or describe your ideal partner.

Wednesday 6th

You may love hanging out with a good friend today and there might be a frisson of romance. Friends could be your escape from a personal issue. Keep close tabs on one friend in particular, especially if you're worried about them. Reach out and make connections.

Thursday 7th

You can get a lot done today, especially when it comes to work and money. Keep your eye on the prize and stoke up your motivation levels with a new financial goal. Show someone at work that you mean business and step in to help. Being willing could impress the boss.

Friday 8th

If you want to book a holiday or sign up for a course of study, go for it this weekend. If you know you're a procrastinator, it's even more important to trust your instincts. Leave it too late and you could lose out on the best deals. Good news from abroad might make your day.

Saturday 9th

A partnership is significant for you this weekend so make time for it. Be open to exploring new events together as fresh input could revive your relationship. It's a good weekend to explore big ideas and experiment with beliefs, religion or philosophy.

Sunday 10th

If you're feeling passionate, throw caution to the wind and let someone know. If you're in a relationship or married, it's a lovely weekend to give in to love and indulge each other. Things may not work out later on today, but for the rest of the time, do more of what you love.

Monday 11th

Pay close attention to money and finances today. There's a new moon on the horizon which is always a good time to initiate new beginnings. Decide what you want to achieve financially over the next year or even longer. Be audacious and draw up a long-term plan.

Tuesday 12th

This is a positive time to focus on money and finances. Budget for the month ahead. You might want to agree on expenses for the festive season, especially if it saves you money. Check your outgoings to see where the better deals are.

Wednesday 13th

Mercury turns retrograde today in your travel and study zone. If you are trying to get away over the next few weeks, be flexible. Know that some of your plans will work out but other plans could fall by the wayside. You may change your mind about an educational course.

Thursday 14th

Taking time out during this Mercury retrograde phase could be helpful. You may find this an exceptionally creative and fertile phase. It would be a good time to follow your spiritual path and explore the metaphysical realm up until the end of the year.

Friday 15th

Try not to get frustrated if plans are going awry. You may need to make an about-turn to accommodate your partner or other people's needs. You could become obsessed with a project and lose track of time. That may mean working late in the office as you play catch up.

Saturday 16th

The moon is in your career zone for the next couple of days, which is unusual at this time of year. Perhaps you're trying to clear the decks if you're taking a longer break over the festive period. Alternatively, you may be caught up on the computer for personal reasons.

Sunday 17th

Trying to make the sums add up could take you down a proverbial rabbit hole. It's not an easy time to get on top of finances and know where you stand. If you're sorting things out financially with a friend, be aware that their money management may be askew.

Monday 18th

You may be presented with a second chance that's linked to travel or study. If you're waiting to hear from someone who lives abroad, it's worth chasing things up. Ideally, put off making a major decision or investment until early January, but do check out what occurs today.

Tuesday 19th

Your sound business head may be required now to sort out a financial mess or muddle. If you're out shopping, take extra care of your money and hold on to receipts in case you need to change anything. It would be easy to lose track of how much you're spending.

Wednesday 20th

If you've been burning the candle at both ends, life could step in to slow you down. You might be flagging if you're at work or you're at home and trying to get the house ready for the holidays. A conversation first thing could deflate your ego – try not to read too much into it.

Thursday 21st

Today's stars are exciting and could bring someone new into your life. Or, they might trigger the opposite scenario and you split up or fall out with someone close. One way or another, relationships could prove lively. Switch off from an online argument and don't be drawn in.

Friday 22nd

The moon is in your star sign restoring your confidence and hopefully boosting your energy levels. Plus, it's the solstice and a new season begins. If you're knocking off work ready for the festive season, you're in tune with your stars. Enjoy yourself and go wild.

Saturday 23rd

It's important to get the right people on your side now. Look out for an expert who can guide you and pay close attention to the people in your life who aren't being helpful. In fact, you could already have moved on from someone who recently let you down.

Sunday 24th

If you're abroad this Christmas Eve visiting an old friend, you're in tune with your stars. If you're at home, you might be last-minute shopping. There could be someone you really want to impress.

Monday 25th

Prioritise love today and you won't go far wrong. It is beautifully romantic astrology and you'll be the happiest spending the day with the one you love. There could be a marriage proposal. Even if you're celebrating with family, ensure you catch up with a loved one.

Tuesday 26th

Avoid the sales like the plague. Not only would it be exhausting but you're unlikely to find anything you want. Try not to get into an argument about money either and resolve to talk about finances another day. Full moon vibes could make for an emotional day.

Wednesday 27th

Whether you're reconnecting with friends or enjoying the potential of social media, reach out and unite with others. New faces and new places are an integral part of today's full moon package. It's about being in the world and not apart from it. Visit the neighbours or catch up with a sibling.

Thursday 28th

Your indulgent nature could kick in today and lead you into trouble. You might have your drinking hat on and be enjoying all the festive parties and get-togethers. Alternatively, you could be in the mood to spend money or make an investment. Try and hold off doing so for a few days yet.

Friday 29th

This could be a promising time for love when someone's got your back. It's a good weekend to focus on your close relationships and look to the future together. The more you share finances and resources equally, the better for everyone involved. This includes family and good friends.

Saturday 30th

Money matters are under the cosmic spotlight and you may be keen to chase up money owed or a past favour. It's a good day to sit down with family and plan the year ahead together. Line up some new financial goals. Work at being more of a tight unit and less independent.

Sunday 31st

Lucky Jupiter switches direction in your star sign on New Year's Eve. This could coincide with a glorious turn of events. Look out for a new opportunity that comes your way and get ready to say yes. If you're looking for love, ensure you're at the biggest party you can find.

Taurus

. . . .

PEOPLE WHO SHARE
YOUR SIGN

PEOPLE WHO SHARE YOUR SIGN

. . . .

Ambitious Taureans dominate in their professional fields, and their tenacity has seen many rise to fame throughout history to the present day. From famous singers like Adele and Ella Fitzgerald, to top models such as Gigi Hadid and renowned film-makers like George Lucas, the beauty that Taureans bring into the world is evident. Discover the creative Taureans who share your exact birthday and see if you can spot any similarities.

21st April

Jessey Stevens (1992), James McAvoy (1979), Steve Backshall (1973), Robert Smith (1959), Iggy Pop (1947), Diana Darvey (1945), Queen Elizabeth II of the United Kingdom (1926), Charlotte Brontë (1816)

22nd April

Louis Smith (1989), Tyra Sanchez (1988), Michelle Ryan (1984), Daniel Johns (1973), Jack Nicholson (1937), Glen Campbell (1936), Immanuel Kant (1724), Queen Isabella I of Castile (1451)

23rd April

Gigi Hadid (1995), Taio Cruz (1980), Jaime King (1979), John Cena (1977), Kal Penn (1977), Michael Moore (1954), Sandra Dee (1942), Shirley Temple (1928), Dorian Leigh (1917), James Buchanan, U.S. President (1791), William Shakespeare (1564)

24th April

Casper Lee (1994), Joe Keery (1992), Kelly Clarkson (1982), Austin Nichols (1980), Cedric the Entertainer (1964), Barbra Streisand (1942), Shirley MacLaine (1934)

25th April

Joslyn Davis (1982), Alejandro Valverde (1980), Tim Duncan (1976), Renée Zellweger (1969), Hank Azaria (1964), Len Goodman (1944), Al Pacino (1940), Ella Fitzgerald (1917), Oliver Cromwell (1599)

26th April

Luke Bracey (1989), Jemima Kirke (1985), Channing Tatum (1980), Melania Trump (1970), Kevin James (1965), Giancarlo Esposito (1958), Roger Taylor (1949), Carol Burnett (1933)

27th April

Froy Gutierrez (1998), Jenna Coleman (1986), Patrick Stump (1984), Darcey Bussell (1969), Tess Daly (1969), Coretta Scott King (1927), Ulysses S. Grant, U.S. President (1822)

28th April

Melanie Martinez (1995), Jessica Alba (1981), Penélope Cruz (1974), Bridget Moynahan (1971), Diego Simeone (1970), Jay Leno (1950), Terry Pratchett (1948), Harper Lee (1926), Oskar Schindler (1908), James Monroe, U.S. President (1758)

29th April

Katherine Langford (1996), Kian Egan (1980), Uma Thurman (1970), Kolinda Grabar-Kitarović, Croatian President (1968), Michelle Pfeiffer (1958), Daniel Day-Lewis (1957), Jerry Seinfeld (1954), Willie Nelson (1933)

30th April

Travis Scott (1992), Dianna Agron (1986), Gal Gadot (1985), Kirsten Dunst (1982), Kunal Nayyar (1981), Johnny Galecki (1975), Leigh Francis (1973), Queen Juliana of the Netherlands (1909)

1st May

Caggie Dunlop (1989), Anushka Sharma (1988), Leonardo Bonucci (1987), Jamie Dornan (1982), James Murray (1976), Wes Anderson (1969), Tim McGraw (1967), Joanna Lumley (1946), Calamity Jane (1852)

2nd May

Lily Allen (1985), Ellie Kemper (1980), David Beckham (1975), Dwayne Johnson (1972), Donatella Versace (1955), Christine Baranski (1952), James Dyson (1947), Catherine the Great (1729)

3rd May

MC Pedrinho (2002), Poppy Delevingne (1986), Rebecca Hall (1982), Eric Church (1977), Christina Hendricks (1975), Rob Brydon (1965), Frankie Valli (1934), James Brown (1933)

4th May

Alex Lawther (1995), Rory McIlroy (1989), Radja Nainggolan (1988), Francesc Fàbregas (1987), Trisha Krishnan (1983), Will Arnett (1970), Keith Haring (1958), Mick Mars (1951), Audrey Hepburn (1929)

5th May

Adele (1988), Brooke Hogan (1988), Bart Baker (1986), Henry Cavill (1983), Craig David (1981), Vincent Kartheiser (1979), Karl Marx (1818)

6th May

Mateo Kovačić (1994), Naomi Scott (1993), Meek Mill (1987), Chris Paul (1985), Dani Alves (1983), George Clooney (1961), Orson Welles (1915), Sigmund Freud (1856)

7th May

Alexander Ludwig (1992), Earl Thomas (1989), Chiara Ferragni (1987), J Balvin (1985), Breckin Meyer (1974), Michael Rosen (1946), Pyotr Ilyich Tchaikovsky (1840), Johannes Brahms (1833)

8th May

Katy B (1989), Nyle DiMarco (1989), Matt Willis (1983), Stephen Amell (1981), Matthew Davis (1978), Enrique Iglesias (1975), David Attenborough (1926), Harry S. Truman, U.S. President (1884)

9th May

Noah Centineo (1996), Audrina Patridge (1985), Rosario
Dawson (1979), Ghostface Killah (1970), John Corbett (1961),
Billy Joel (1949), Candice Bergen (1946), Albert Finney (1936)

10th May

Halston Sage (1993), Lindsey Shaw (1989), Aslı Enver (1984),
Linda Evangelista (1965), Bono (1960), Ellen Ochoa (1958),
Sid Vicious (1957), Fred Astaire (1899)

11th May

Sabrina Carpenter (1999), Lana Condor (1997), Thibaut
Courtois (1992), Blac Chyna (1988), Holly Valance (1983),
Jonathan Jackson (1982), Cory Monteith (1982), Salvador
Dalí (1904)

12th May

Emily VanCamp (1986), Domhnall Gleeson (1983), Malin
Åkerman (1978), Jason Biggs (1978), Tony Hawk (1968),
Catherine Tate (1968), Emilio Estevez (1962), Florence
Nightingale (1820)

13th May

Romelu Lukaku (1993), Debby Ryan (1993), Tommy Dorfman
(1992), Robert Pattinson (1986), Iwan Rheon (1985), Yaya
Touré (1983), Stevie Wonder (1950), Joe Louis (1914)

14th May

Martin Garrix (1996), Miranda Cosgrove (1993), Dustin Lynch
(1985), Olly Murs (1984), Mark Zuckerberg (1984), Martine
McCutcheon (1976), Cate Blanchett (1969), Greg Davies (1968),
George Lucas (1944)

15th May

Birdy (1996), Sophie Cookson (1990), Stella Maxwell (1990), Andy Murray (1987), Alexandra Breckenridge (1982), Zara Tindall (1981), Ray Lewis (1975), Brian Eno (1948), Madeleine Albright (1937)

16th May

Thomas Brodie-Sangster (1990), Megan Fox (1986), Billy Crawford (1982), Tori Spelling (1973), David Boreanaz (1969), Janet Jackson (1966), Pierce Brosnan (1953), Danny Trejo (1944)

17th May

AJ Mitchell (2001), Ross Butler (1990), Charlotte Crosby (1990), Nikki Reed (1988), Tahj Mowry (1986), Passenger (1984), Kandi Burruss (1976), Jordan Knight (1970), Enya (1961), Bob Saget (1956), Bill Paxton (1955), Gary Paulsen (1939)

18th May

Madilyn Paige (1997), KYLE (1993), Jack Johnson (1975), Tina Fey (1970), Miriam Margolyes (1941), Pope John Paul II (1920), Perry Como (1912), Fred Perry (1909)

19th May

JoJo Siwa (2003), Marshmello (1992), Sam Smith (1992), Eleanor Tomlinson (1992), Lily Cole (1987), Kiera Cass (1981), Yo Gotti (1981), Kevin Garnett (1976), Israel Houghton (1971), Grace Jones (1948), Peter Mayhew (1944), Malcom X (1925)

20th May

Matt Terry (1993), Jon Pardi (1985), Naturi Naughton (1984), Rachel Platten (1981), Busta Rhymes (1972), Mary Pope Osborne (1949), Cher (1946), James Stewart (1908)

21st May

Tom Daley (1994), Mario Mandzukic (1986), Gotye (1980), Noel Fielding (1973), The Notorious B.I.G. (1972), Mark Crilley (1966), Mr. T (1952)